VISUAL GUIDE TO

Fabric Selection to Finishing
Techniques & Beyond

Patchwork &
Quilting

stashBOOKS®

an imprint of C&T Publishing

Text, photography, and artwork copyright © 2017 by C&T Publishing, Inc.

PUBLISHER
Amy Marson

CREATIVE DIRECTOR
Gailen Runge

PROJECT EDITOR
Alice Mace Nakanishi

COMPILER
Lindsay Conner

DEVELOPMENTAL EDITORS
Liz Aneloski, Cynthia Bix, Joanna Burgarino, Stacy Chamness, Phyllis Elving, S. Michele Fry, Carrie Hargrave, Lynn Koolish, Karla Menaugh, Kandy Petersen, Debbie Rodgers, Deb Rowden, Lisa Ruble, and Katie Van Amburg

TECHNICAL EDITORS
Carolyn Aune, Mary E. Flynn, Helen Frost, Ann Haley, Cynthia Hilton, Joyce Lytle, Sara Kate MacFarland, Susan Nelsen, Ellen Pahl, Sandy Peterson, Nan Powell, Debbie Rodgers, Gailen Runge, Amanda Siegfried, Alison M. Schmidt, Teresa Stroin, Julie Waldman, Sadhana Wray, and Nanette S. Zeller

COVER/BOOK DESIGNER
April Mostek

PRODUCTION COORDINATORS
Zinnia Heinzmann and Tim Manibusan

PRODUCTION EDITOR
Jennifer Warren

INDEXER
Amron Gravett, Wild Clover Book Services

ILLUSTRATORS
Freesia Pearson Blizard, Jeff Carrillo, Lon Eric Craven, Jenny Davis, Mary E. Flynn, Valyrie Friedman, Jessica Jenkins, Alan McCorkle, Judith Baker Montano, Kirstie L. Pettersen, Jay Richards, Gretchen Schwarzenbach, Aliza Shalit, Rose Sheifer, Richard Sheppard, Tim Manibusan, and Gregg Valley

PHOTOGRAPHY BY Nissa Brehmer, Christina Carty-Francis, Luke Mulks, and Diane Pedersen, as well as John Bagley, Sharon Risedorph, and Richard Tauber, unless otherwise noted

COVER PHOTOGRAPHY BY
Lucy Glover of C&T Publishing, Inc.

Published by Stash Books, an imprint of C&T Publishing, Inc., P.O. Box 1456, Lafayette, CA 94549

Library of Congress Cataloging-in-Publication Data

Title: Visual guide to patchwork & quilting : fabric selection to finishing techniques & beyond.

Other titles: Visual guide to patchwork and quilting

Description: Lafayette, CA : Stash Books, an imprint of C&T Publishing, Inc., 2017. | Includes index.

Identifiers: LCCN 2017021458 | ISBN 9781617455612 (soft cover)

Subjects: LCSH: Patchwork--Patterns. | Quilting--Patterns.

Classification: LCC TT835 .V57 2017 | DDC 746.46/041--dc23

LC record available at https://lccn.loc.gov/2017021458

Printed in China

10 9 8 7 6 5 4 3 2 1

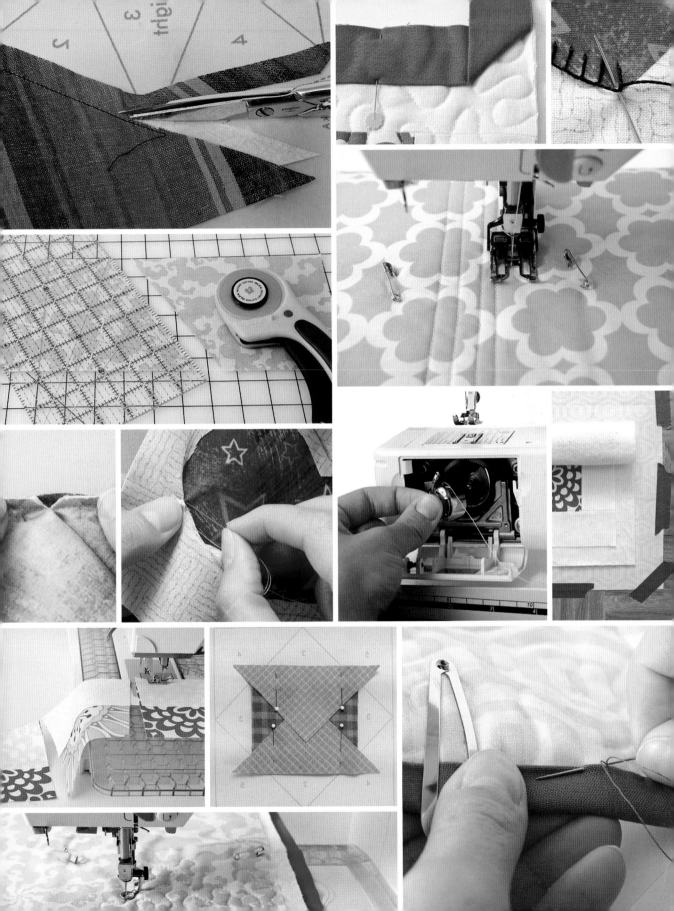

Contents

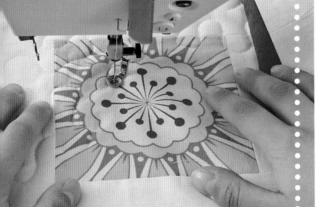

Chapter 1: Quilting Supplies and Tools

These are the basics you need to know to get started, from setting up a simple sewing area to collecting the basic tools. This is the very first step in your quiltmaking adventure.

Setting Up a Sewing Area

BY HARRIET HARGRAVE AND CARRIE HARGRAVE

It may be daunting to think about all the equipment needed to start quilting if you are just beginning. If you already have a sewing room … great! You are ready to jump in and begin. However, while having a dedicated sewing space is nice, be assured that it is not really necessary for making a quilt.

SEWING MACHINE AREA

Piecing does not require an extensive work area like machine quilting does. The rough minimum sewing space you need for making a quilt top is about 3 feet by 4 feet, mostly to your left and behind your sewing machine. If your machine is on a tabletop instead of in a cabinet, you will need a good support system around the machine. If you are sewing on a dining room or kitchen table, the photo shows a great setup for a sewing machine. It is easily taken apart and put away when the space is needed for other things.

Setup of a basic sewing area

IRONING AREA

Your ironing board is a major workstation when you are piecing. Be sure that it is heavy, stable, and not warped. If yours has any of these issues, shop for a new one.

When ironing (even clothing), be aware that too much padding can lead to distortion. When you are piecing a quilt, inaccurate pressing of the pieces can ruin your project. A thin layer of 100% cotton batting (not more than ⅛″ thick) makes an ideal ironing pad under the ironing board cover. A gridded ironing board cover is helpful. If the cover is stretched onto the board tight and straight, the lines of the grid can be used as guides to keep strips straight when pressing.

It can be difficult to handle larger pieces on an ironing board because of its shape. It's helpful to turn the ironing board around so you are working on the wider end.

tip Avoid using a Teflon ironing board cover. The slippery surface makes it hard for the fabric pieces to get a grip and create resistance for the iron. Also, the fabric does not dry after you have steamed or starched it. Cotton is preferable because cotton sticks to cotton and absorbs moisture, and a cotton ironing board cover will keep the pieces from sliding when you are ironing seams. It also allows the pieces to dry quickly between steaming and starching.

CUTTING AREA

Kitchen or laundry room counters, or even the top of the clothes dryer, are good places to set up a makeshift cutting area. Just make sure it's not too far from your sewing and ironing area.

Find a place that's at a comfortable height. If you are over 5 feet tall, about 36″ is the best height. If you are under 5 feet tall, 32″ or less will work for you. The main idea is that you do not want to lean over too much (ideally not at all) in order to be comfortable and to have the strength and power to cut the fabric cleanly and accurately.

Sewing Machines

BY HARRIET HARGRAVE AND CARRIE HARGRAVE

Of course, if you are going to learn to machine piece, you need a sewing machine. Today's sewing machine companies put a great deal of effort into making machines (even midline machines) that do everything, from straight stitch to digitized embroidery. The real story is that to excel at machine piecing, appliqué, and quilting, you need only a very basic machine. Few stitches beyond straight stitches are required, but there are some basic things you should consider when choosing a machine.

CHOOSING A SEWING MACHINE

We strongly advise you to avoid buying a cheap sewing machine at a big box store. It is best to choose a quality machine that not only gives you the features you need to start out but also allows you to grow into other techniques.

An excellent way to get a high-quality machine at an affordable price is to look for a good used machine. The used machines of today were the top-end machines of a few years ago. A reliable sewing machine dealer generally has trade-in

machines that are worth looking at. Try to test drive as many models and brands as you can, and make sure you actually sew on the machine you like best before you buy it. Many newer computerized machines are difficult for new sewers to understand, and you will be frustrated because the machine is in control instead of you!

If you don't want to invest in a machine, borrowing one from a family member or a friend is a good way to get started. If you already have a machine (or you borrow one), take it to a qualified mechanic and have it cleaned, oiled, and adjusted.

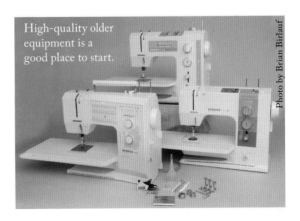

High-quality older equipment is a good place to start.

Photo by Brian Birlauf

When you choose a machine, make sure that it is easy to regulate and understand. As you test it, note the sound of the machine, the placement of your foot on the foot control, the way the fabric feeds through the machine while you are sewing, the brightness of the machine light, and the machine's functions and accessories. Following are some functions and accessories that we recommend:

- *Fully adjustable stitch width and length capabilities.* Many machines have stitch length and width settings in predefined increments. This can hinder the ability to adjust the machine to any setting you need or want. A dial that has infinite settings between the numbers is ideal.

- *A bobbin with a case that inserts from the front of the machine* instead of dropping in from the top. These bobbin cases are more easily adjustable than the top, drop-in models. Placement of a seam guide can be a problem with a drop-in system. Also consider bobbin size: the more thread it holds, the better.

- *A top tension adjustment dial that is easily accessible.* Numbers on the dial are also necessary.

- *Presser feet that change easily* and are stable (that do not wobble on the shank).

- *A feed-dog drop system that is easily accessible.*

- *A good-sized work surface around the machine,* or a tightly fitting portable sewing table that is made to go with the machine.

- *A foot control* that is at a comfortable angle for your foot, so you can maintain control of the speed for long periods.

- *Presser feet and accessories* that really do the job:

  ¼″ foot

  Straight-stitch foot

  Seam guide bar

  Open-toe appliqué foot

  ¼″ round free-motion (darning) foot

  ¼″ round open-toe free-motion foot

  Walking foot

  Straight-stitch throat plate

PRESSER FEET

The importance of presser feet cannot be overstated. They affect your view as you sew, the feeding of the fabric, and the accuracy of your seams. Most sewing machines come with a variety of presser feet, but most of these are for dressmaking and do not work for the narrow seam allowances used in patchwork.

In the past few years, we have seen presser feet developed especially for piecing ¼″ seams. A universal ¼″ foot is the Little Foot, developed by Lynn Graves. This foot is designed to be a perfect ¼″ on the right side of the needle. The foot has ¼″ markings on the side to indicate the needle position: ¼″ behind the needle for starting the seam; a line directly across from the needle; and ¼″ in front of the needle, to indicate when to stop ¼″ from the edge. This foot is available in several shank sizes to adapt to most machines and is a good choice if your machine does not have a ¼″ foot available.

Various ¼″ piecing feet

Most sewing machine companies have made ¼″ feet for their specific brands for several years now, and the theory is that on all ¼″ feet, it's exactly ¼″ from the needle to the right-hand edge of the presser foot. However, because these feet aren't necessarily totally accurate, not all quilters like using them.

NOTE *Not all sewing machines have this foot available because the manufacturers have made their straight-stitch feet wide like zigzag feet, with a single hole where the needle passes through. This foot does not meet our needs.*

STRAIGHT-STITCH THROAT PLATE

The throat plate is the metal piece that surrounds the feed dog. The standard throat plate on a modern machine has an oval opening that accommodates a zigzag stitch, which doesn't work well for piecing. The oval hole allows the needle to push fabric down with it, and the stitch may not be made cleanly. Also, strips tend to veer away from the edge of the seam guide as you approach the ends, so it is hard to keep them straight and even while sewing. A straight-stitch plate will help eliminate this problem. This plate's opening is too small to allow the fabric to enter with the needle. Straight-stitch machines such as Singer Featherweights make perfect stitches, and many quilters still prefer to piece on their old machines because of the stitch quality.

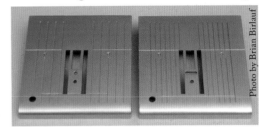

Straight-stitch and zigzag throat plates

Rotary Cutters and Cutting Mats

BY HARRIET HARGRAVE AND CARRIE HARGRAVE

The variety of rotary cutters and mats available today is amazing. When Harriet started quilting in the 1970s, rotary cutters had not been invented yet! Once they hit the market in the early 1980s, they revolutionized cutting fabric for quilting.

ROTARY CUTTERS

A rotary cutter is like a round razor blade with a handle. Rotary cutters are available in 18 mm, 28 mm, 45 mm, 60 mm, and 65 mm blade sizes. There are several brands of rotary cutters, each with slightly different features. We suggest that you go to various quilting stores and ask to test-drive the brands and styles of cutters they carry. You will find that there is a vast difference in how they are held and where the pressure is applied as you cut with them.

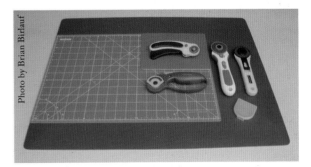

Rotary cutting supplies

Cutting fabric correctly is critical to good piecing, and cutting is where beginners have the most difficulty. If your cutter does not fit your hand properly, or you can't apply even and steady pressure to the blade for the entire length of the cut, the cut will not go through the fabric layers and/or the edge will not be cut cleanly.

NOTE *Please don't let the preferences of your friends, your mom or grandma, or a salesclerk influence what you buy. Try what they like and recommend, but form your own opinion after trying several different cutters.*

We recommend starting with the 45 mm size. It is easy to cut with, goes through four layers of fabric easily, rides above the thickness of a rotary ruler, and comes in models with many different shapes and handles. This is the only size you need to get started.

NOTE **SAFETY!** *Be very careful when using rotary cutters. They are razor sharp! Make it a habit to close your cutter every time you lay it down. Never leave a cutter lying around, open or closed, where small children can get hold of it.*

Holding a Cutter Properly

Many books, as well as the instructions on cutter packages, suggest that you hold the cutter with a closed fist. This method doesn't help direct the energy of your arm and hand onto the blade. Instead, let the handle of the cutter rest comfortably in the palm of your hand. Your index finger should extend forward, resting on the grooved space at the top edge of the handle (if the cutter has this). Your thumb should be on one side of the handle, and the other three fingers should curl gently around the other side.

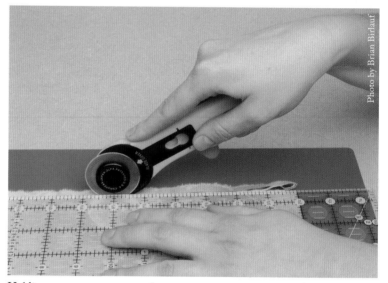

Holding a rotary cutter properly

Always cut *away* from your body. The muscles you use when pushing are stronger than those you use when pulling. You also eliminate the possibility of losing control of the cutter and hurting yourself!

Maintenance

The rotary cutter blade is razor sharp when new, but after dozens of cuts it can start to dull. A dull blade requires more force than a sharp blade to do the same work, which can be tiring and can make your cutting inaccurate. Make sure you have one or two new blades on hand.

Several newer cutters on the market have easy blade-changing systems. When changing the blade on one of the other cutters, lay out the parts in the order you take them off the handle. Wipe any lint from the back of the handle area that the blade rests on. Change the blade, making sure you select only a single blade if you purchased a multipack, and reassemble the parts in reverse order. You will notice that the new blade has a thin film of oil on it. Do not wipe this off, because it helps lubricate the blade while cutting.

Lay out parts of cutter in order as you disassemble it.

ROTARY CUTTING MATS

The cutting surface is just as important as the cutter you use. The mat allows you to press down on the cutter and let the blade sink slightly into the surface of the mat. Rotary cutting mats come in different sizes and materials, so you'll need to try a few to find your preferences as to thickness, hardness, and ease of cutting.

- Three-layer mats (made by Elan and OLFA) are made of two layers of PVC plastic, with a softer center layer. They are "self-healing," meaning that the cuts do not stay in the surface. Either side can be cut on. Store them flat and away from heat; they will warp if exposed to a heat source or left in a hot car.

- The harder, thinner version of the three-layer mat (made by OLFA, Omnigrid, and Ginger) feels flatter and harder when cutting. This type is also self-healing, and either side can be used to cut.

- Soft plastic mats are solid translucent white plastic with a textured side (the cutting side) and a smooth side. They are usually not self-healing—the cutter may leave marks on the surface. Cuts can be smoothed with emery cloth or very fine sandpaper, but over time the board can become grooved and will distort the path of your cutter. It also dulls blades faster.

- A few mats (made by June Tailor and Fiskars) are very hard plastic and have a textured cutting surface. Only one side of these mats can be used for cutting, and, of all the mats, these seem to be the hardest to cut accurately on.

Rotary mats come in a variety of sizes. The most versatile size, 18˝ × 24˝, is what we recommend to start. If or when you get a large cutting table, the 24˝ × 36˝ mat is more efficient for doing a lot of cutting. There are also small mats that are handy for quick trimming at the machine and for taking to classes. Finally, there are mats that attach to ironing surfaces for use in very confined spaces.

Working Without the Grid Lines

All mats come with a 1˝ grid printed on one side. Many books will tell you to work with this grid, but rarely do the mat lines match the lines of your ruler, and you will have too many lines to look at. Therefore, work on the solid side only, and rely on your ruler for accurate measurements.

Ruler Basics

BY HARRIET HARGRAVE AND CARRIE HARGRAVE

Along with rotary cutters and cutting mats, rulers make up the foundation of the rotary revolution. A clear, accurate ruler is as important to guiding the cutter as a sharp blade is to cutting. There are many different rulers available for both general and specialty use. Rotary rulers are made of thick, clear acrylic and have lines and numbers evenly spaced across them. The number of lines and their spacing varies between brands, as do the color and thickness of the lines. Rulers that have numbers running in both directions are easy for both right- and left-handed quilters to use.

RULER BRANDS AND CHARACTERISTICS

When deciding on a ruler brand, keep the following in mind:

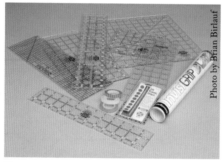

Variety of rulers in basic sizes

- *Do not change brands of rulers in the middle of a project!* We cannot stress enough how important this point is. The measurements marked on the different brands will vary slightly. Find a brand you like, and stick with it.

- Make sure that the brand you choose comes in a fairly large selection of sizes and shapes.

- Be sure to place the rulers on top of both dark and light fabrics to check that the color of the lines shows enough to enable you to work with the ruler easily and accurately.

- Check the thickness of the printed lines. The thicker the line, the greater the chance that you will measure and cut inaccurately.

- It is handy to have a ruler marked with a 45°-angle line, as well as 30°- and 60°-angle lines.

- Some brands have a ½″ measure on one side and end. Be sure to keep this in mind when cutting. The ½″ is added so that you only have to think about the finished strip size you need—the ½″ seam allowance is already added. This can cause trouble if you don't pay attention to it.

BASIC STARTER SIZES

To start with, you will need a limited number of rulers. Good sizes to start with are any combination of the following:

- 2½″ × 12½″

- 3½″ × 18½″

- 4″ × 12″ (or 4″ × 14″)

- 6½″ × 12″ (or 6½″ × 18½″)

- 6½″ square

- 9½″ square

- 12½″ square

- 18½″ square

NOTE *Some brands add a ½″ measure to two sides of their rulers; others do not. The sizes in the following paragraph are the general sizes of the rulers, whether the ½″ is added or not. Creative Grids all have ½″ added. Some Omnigrid rulers do and some don't. It would be advisable to be consistent in this when buying rulers.*

The four "bare-bones" basic sizes you will need to make most quilts are:

2½″ × 12½″   6½″ × 12″ (or 6½″ × 18½″)

4″ × 12″ (or 4″ × 14″)   6½″ square

Add the other sizes once you get into adding borders, and for continuing in your quilting.

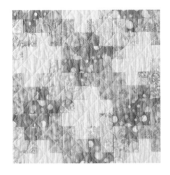

ACCURATE MEASURING GUIDES

Before investing in a ruler, test-drive several brands and sizes, especially to see how well you can read them. Many quilters find that certain color markings or too many lines make cutting very confusing and fatiguing. Be sure that you can easily read the measurements and follow a line the length of the ruler without your eyes blurring. (Confusion in reading the lines will lead to inaccurate cutting.) Strips of self-stick plastic called Glow-Line Tape can be placed along a measure line to help you with ruler placement.

SLIPPAGE-STOP PRODUCTS

Ruler slippage is a common problem when cutting. Quilter's Rule rulers have a molded side with a raised grid to prevent slippage. Creative Grid rulers have built-in grips on the back along the sides.

Some products can be placed on the back of any ruler. Invisi-Grip by Omnigrid "disappears" but stops a lot of the slippage. Fabric Grips by Collins are small sandpaper circles with self-adhesive backing. EZ Clear Fabric Grabbers are clear, but thicker. They really grab the fabric, but they make the ruler sit above the surface of the fabric.

If you don't want something permanently stuck to your ruler, you can use small pieces of plastic shelf liner or rug backing. These stick to the ruler when you apply pressure but peel off easily.

We have found that slippage often occurs when using a ruler that is wider than needed. Use the narrowest ruler you can for the size of strips you are cutting, and slippage will be less of a problem.

Threads

BY HARRIET HARGRAVE AND CARRIE HARGRAVE

Right up front, we will state that you need to use only 100% cotton thread when piecing. When polyester fabrics were introduced years ago, polyester threads were needed for strength and stretchability. This thread overtook the market, and 100% cotton thread was difficult to obtain.

Once quilting took off in the 1980s, however, cotton thread became king again. We are now facing the polyester problem anew, as some thread companies are trying to push polyester on us again—to the serious detriment of our quilts in the years ahead.

Consider these facts when selecting threads:

- Threads and fabrics need to be of like fibers—for example, natural-fiber fabrics should be sewn with natural-fiber threads.

- The thread should be weaker than the fabric. Thread that is too strong will cut and weaken the fabric in the seam, causing the fabric to "break." If a thread breaks in a seam, the seam can be mended; if the fabric tears, it cannot be mended.

- Thread size should be as fine as possible, but it should always be consistent with the strength requirement of the seam. Finer threads tend to become buried below the surface of the fabric and are subjected to less abrasion than seams with heavier thread, which are on top of the fabric. Finer threads also require smaller needles, producing less fabric distortion than heavier needles do.

NOTE ▶ **WARNING!** *When piecing, do not buy 50/2 or 60/2 threads, such as Aurifil, DMC, or Mettler Fine Embroidery thread. These are machine embroidery threads and are too weak for the stresses of pieced seams. These threads are good for paper piecing with a shortened stitch length, for appliqué, for machine embroidery, and for very close machine quilting.*

- The preferred thread size for sewing cotton quilting fabric is 50/3. The "50" is the yarn count of the thread, or its weight and diameter. The "3" is the number of plies twisted together. The higher the first number, the finer the thread. The more plies, the stronger the thread. A newer thread has been introduced: 60/3, which is finer than the 50 but almost as strong because of the three plies. Because it is finer, a smaller needle can be used, giving nicer-quality stitches. It also accommodates the ¼″ seam allowance better, as it takes up less space in the seam.

tip The Slide Test

Here is Carrie's great way for testing whether your thread fits the eye of your needle: Thread a machine needle with a length of thread. Hold the thread in front of you horizontally. Tip one end of the thread at a 45° angle. If the needle doesn't move, the eye is too small; try a larger needle. If the needle flies down the thread, the eye is too large; try a smaller needle. If the needle skips easily down the thread, you have found the needle size to stitch with; just double-check for stitch quality.

Photo by Brian Birlauf

Testing needle size

- Thread strength should be less than that of the fabric to be sewn. Authorities agree that the seam strength should be about 60%–70% of the fabric strength. The reason for this is if excessive stress is placed on a seam, the thread in the seam will break instead of the fabric. Cotton thread is weaker than cotton fabric; polyester thread is not. In addition, polyester thread has tiny, abrasive edges that work as saw blades against the soft cotton fibers, and cut through the seams over time.

- When purchasing cotton threads, unroll a length and check for quality. A fuzzy thread is made from short fibers, rendering it weak and giving it poor sewing properties. Finding uneven areas, called *slubs*, is another indication of a lower-quality thread. A thread with very few or no fuzzy ends is generally made from long fibers. This thread will sew a nicer seam and will last longer in the finished seam.

Needles

BY HARRIET HARGRAVE AND CARRIE HARGRAVE

The sewing machine needle is probably the number one cause of problems for sewers. It is the first thing to check when you are experiencing stitch problems. High-quality needles are critical to achieving smooth, even stitches. *Use the needle type, size, and brand recommended for your machine.* In addition, use a needle that complements your thread choice. Always start each project with a new needle. We can't stress enough that not only your understanding of needles and thread but also your choices about them will directly affect whether your machine sews to the best of its ability.

PARTS OF A NEEDLE

Examine a large machine needle, such as a 100/16 (see the illustration, above right). Notice that the needle is flat on the backside of the shank and has a long thread groove on the opposite side. The flat shank provides perfect positioning of the needle in the needle bar and in relation to the point of the hook. Run your fingernail down the groove. This groove protects the thread within the needle as it penetrates the fabric. The thread slides through the grooved side and the eye. When a stitch is formed, the thread is pinched between the fabric and the needle, creating a loop behind the needle as the needle rises. This loop and the scarf (the hollowed-out area on the back of the needle) allow the hook point of the shuttle to pass between the thread and the needle, locking the stitch.

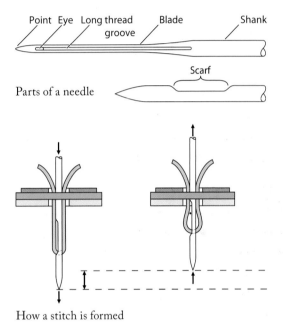

Parts of a needle

How a stitch is formed

NEEDLE BRANDS

Schmetz is one of the most recognized needle brands on the market, but it does not fit every machine. Klasse is another commonly found brand that is very similar to Schmetz. If you have a Singer, especially an older one, make sure that you use Singer brand needles. Janome recommends that Organ needles be used in its machines. Different brand needles have a different position for the eye, a different length from the eye to the point, and/or a different scarf on the back of the needle that affects the machine's ability to stitch properly.

Various brands of needles

The information that you need in order to choose the correct needle is printed on the front of the needle packet. We are using Schmetz packages as an example. Different letters and numbers may be used on different needle brands; be sure to familiarize yourself with your machine's requirements. Needles sold for industrial machines use a completely different system. On a Schmetz package, under the brand name is the type of needle, referring to the type of point the needle has—universal, topstitching, jeans/denim, microtex, and so forth. Below that is a series of numbers, which refer to the needle shank shape and the length and shape of the needle's point. The first set of numbers refers to the needle system. For example, in 130/705, the "130" is the shank length, and the "705" indicates that it is a flat shank. These numbers will help you determine which needle system is suitable for your machine.

The first letter after the numbers refers to needle scarf (e.g., H indicates needle scarf, B indicates no needle scarf). The next letter indicates the type of needle point (M = sharp, J = denim, Q = quilting, E = embroidery, and so on). The shank of the needle is also often marked with a color to help you identify the type of point once the needle is removed from the packet.

The needle size is indicated in both metric and U.S. sizes. The metric number represents the needle diameter (size 70/10 = 0.7 mm). This set of numbers will help you determine the needle's suitability for a given fabric, thread size, or sewing process.

Needle packet information

The universal point needle, which has a slightly rounded point, has long been the standard sewing machine needle. The newer sharp microtex needles were developed to sew silk, microfibers, and other new textiles that require a sharp piercing point to prevent puckered seams. These new needles are also excellent for topstitching, which requires a very straight line of visible stitches. The universal needle performs beautifully for sewing patchwork seams at a much lower cost than the microtex needles, which wear down quickly and must be changed more often than universals. As a beginner, it may be difficult for you to see a difference in the stitch quality of the two different needles. However, try sewing a seam using each needle type to see which you prefer. We recommend that you stick with universals unless you are sewing batik fabrics, which require a microtex needle.

As for size, the needle, thread, and fabric all need to marry together. The needle carries the thread through the fabric; therefore, the hole made by the needle must be large enough to accommodate the thread size. The thread groove should be deep enough to allow the thread to lie in it. The needle eye must also be the right size. If it is too small for the thread to pass through, the thread will fray and break, and stitches will be skipped. If the thread is too fine for the needle, the hole made by the needle will not be filled by the thread, resulting in a weak and unsightly seam. The more room the thread has to flop around in the eye, the harder it is on the thread.

The Needle/Thread Reference chart (below) gives corresponding needle and thread sizes to assist you in choosing a needle for the thread size and fabric weight you are sewing. As a general guide, start with the smallest needle size recommended for your thread weight and ply. If the thread breaks or skips stitches, go to the next larger size.

NEEDLE/THREAD REFERENCE

Thread size	Needle size							
	60	65	70	75	80	90	100	110
Ultra fine thread 80/2	●	●						
Nylon monofilament thread	●	●	●	●	●			
Fine machine embroidery thread 60/2		●	●	●				
Machine embroidery thread 50/2		●	●	●				
Embroidery thread 30/2			●	●	●			
Merc. cotton sewing thread 60/3			●	●				
Merc. cotton sewing thread 50/3				●	●			
Synthetic sewing thread (spun)				●	●			
Cotton-wrapped polyester thread						●		
Cotton hand quilting thread						●	●	
Buttonhole (cordonnet) thread							●	●

Sewing for Accuracy

BY HARRIET HARGRAVE AND CARRIE HARGRAVE

CHOOSING A SEAM GUIDE

You have several options, from simple, homemade guides to manufactured ones. These guides will provide a barrier for the edge of the fabric to glide against.

Masking tape   Harriet's students have great success using layers of ¼˝ masking tape, available at quilt stores. An ⅛˝-thick section of tape 2˝ long secured to the throat plate and bed of your machine will create an excellent barrier guide to run the fabric edge against. (Make deep cuts into the roll of tape, and peel off a thick section between the cuts.) Place the tape in front of the right toe of the foot, especially if the foot is too wide for the seam allowance you need to use.

Using ¼˝ masking tape as seam guide

Straight-stitch foot   Harriet's favorite foot, the BERNINA #13 straight-stitch foot, has a guide bar that attaches to the foot. It makes sewing perfect seams easy, once you have positioned it accurately. After the guide bar is in position, the extra arm of the guide bar that extends to the left can be cut off to about ¾˝.

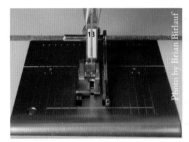

BERNINA seam guide sits on top of right feed dog.

Mole foam   This adhesive padding, made to protect pressure points on people's feet, is also a commonly used seam guide. Use a ruler and a rotary cutter with an old blade inserted to cut the foam sheet into ¼˝ × 2˝ strips. Expose the adhesive, and position the strips on the bed of the machine. The only drawback to mole foam is that a groove will wear into the side over time. Keep an eye on this, and replace the foam as necessary, or your piecing can become inaccurate.

Other guides Two-piece guides that screw into the bed of the machine have long been available. They are very accurate, and vibration from the machine never moves them out of place. Magnetic guides are available from various manufacturers, but they have drawbacks. Vibration can move them slightly, and they won't work on a machine with a plastic bed unless there is a large metal throat-plate area. If you have a computerized machine, check with your dealer to make sure this kind of guide can be used.

Photo by Brian Birlauf

Various seam guides

STITCH LENGTH

Once you have chosen a foot and placed a seam guide on your machine, you will need to set the machine to a stitch length that will give you a secure seam but will be long enough to rip out if necessary. It is important that you understand a little about stitch length and know the minimum, average, and maximum stitch length your machine can produce.

Your machine measures stitch length in either millimeters or stitches per inch. Most of the newer machines have stitch lengths measured in millimeters. Here is a basic guideline for what your machine is telling you if it measures in millimeters: 6mm equals about ¼″, so if you have the stitch length set at 6, your stitches will be about ¼″ long. Another way to think about it is that if your machine is set at 2, then the stitches will measure 2mm long, and if we know that 6mm equals about ¼″, then 2mm stitches are about $\frac{1}{12}$″, or 12 stitches to the inch.

This chart shows you how these two measurements compare.

We recommend that you set the stitch length between 12 and 14 stitches per inch, or 1.75 to 2 on a machine measuring in millimeters. This length will yield a secure seam and will allow you to slip a seam-ripper blade easily under a single stitch if you need to rip out a seam. Sew a couple of seams to see which stitch length you prefer.

Stitches per inch	Millimeters (mm)
50	0.5
25	1
16	1.5
12	2
10	2.5

Beyond the Basic Supplies

BY ALEX ANDERSON

Quilters love gadgets, and every year more tools and notions are introduced to the quiltmaking world. Your first visit to a quilt shop or the quilting section of a fabric store can be overwhelming. There are many decisions to make when purchasing the necessary tools to get started. The following list includes the basics for a well-stocked sewing space.

Pins Don't skimp on these! My favorites are extra-fine (1⅜″/0.5 mm) glass-head pins. I use them for piecing and appliqué. They're a bit pricey but well worth the investment, especially if you stock up when the good ones go on sale. Avoid large, bargain-brand quilting pins for piecing and appliqué; not only can they get in your way and tangle with your thread, but also their thickness can throw off the accuracy of your seams.

You'll also want pins to use for temporarily securing the layers of your quilt sandwich for basting in preparation for hand quilting. (Eventually, you'll replace them with thread.) For machine quilting, rustproof size #1 safety pins are a good choice. The colored ones are extremely pliable, easy to see … and fun!

Marking tools There are lots of options for marking on fabric, but my personal favorites are silver pencils (there are many brands available) and extrahard-lead mechanical pencils. If the pencil says "verithin" it just means a very thin lead. These simple tools allow me to mark a nice, fine line; they show up on most fabrics; and all their marks are fairly easy to remove with gentle washing. Another popular option is Pilot's FriXion pen, which doesn't require washing to remove. A water-soluble pen can be useful for marking quilts for machine quilting (although I avoid this type of marker for hand quilting, where it may leave a residue that's tough to quilt through). If you use a water-soluble marker, be sure to *follow the manufacturer's instructions carefully*, and be aware that you must be willing and able to immerse the finished quilt in cold water to remove the markings. The markings from these pens are also very sensitive to heat, so never press the marked quilt top until the markings have been removed.

tip Always test your intended marking tool on a sample of your fabric before marking to make sure the marks come out.

Stiletto and seam ripper

A stiletto is a sharply pointed tool that you'll find helpful for coaxing turn-under allowances on appliqués and for controlling small pieces as you feed them through the sewing machine. A seam ripper … well, even a seasoned quilter needs one from time to time. My 4-in-1 Essential Sewing

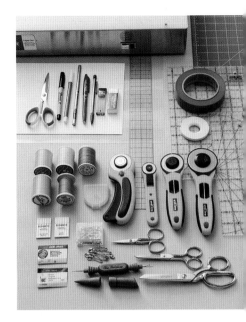

Tool (by C&T Publishing) includes a stiletto and a seam ripper, plus a pointed end for turning under fabric edges, as well as a handy pressing tool.

4-in-1 Essential Sewing Tool

¼″- and 1″-wide masking tape

This tape comes in handy for marking straight lines and grids for quilting, taping layers in preparation for basting, and many other basic sewing-room tasks. Another option is blue painter's tape; although it comes in a limited number of widths, it doesn't leave residue as masking tape is sometimes wont to do.

Fine-lead mechanical pencil and eraser You'll use this versatile pencil for dozens of sewing-room tasks. As to the eraser: We all make mistakes once in awhile!

Black, permanent, felt-tip pen You'll find many uses for a fine-tip permanent marker in the sewing room.

Heat-resistant template material: For shapes that must be traced multiple times, both for piecing and appliqué, it's a good idea to make a template from sturdy material. While cardboard or card stock will work, a much better choice is the translucent template plastic available at your local quilt shop. Choose a heavier, heat-resistant variety for appliqué, particularly for circles.

Lightbox or light table A lightbox provides a light source that will enable you to transfer your quilting motifs onto the quilt top and to trace and position appliqués. Any flat, clear, backlit surface will work. Commercial lightboxes are available, but I prefer a larger surface to work on. My light "box" is an 18˝ × 36˝ piece of ¼˝-thick, clear Plexiglas. When it's time to trace, I set it between two chairs and place a lamp on the floor beneath it. If you have a dining room table that extends with leaves, consider getting the Plexiglas cut a couple of inches larger that the size of the leaves. Extend your table, substitute the Plexiglas for the leaves, and place a lamp on the floor beneath. You can also substitute a sunny window or place a lamp or flashlight beneath a glass-topped table.

HINTS FOR ACCURATE SEWING

Here are a few things to check when setting up your sewing machine:

- Check your **body position** when sitting at your machine. You should be facing the presser foot straight on when you align the fabric with the edge of the foot. If your body is angled, your perception of the edge of the fabric and the edge of the foot will be incorrect, and your seams will be less accurate.

- Be aware of the **time of day** and the **position of the light** around your work. If you start piecing in the morning with natural light on your left side and finish up at night with artificial light above you, your eyes are apt to see the edge of the foot differently. Keep the light consistent at all times if possible.

- Check that the **foot is stable** on the machine. Many clip-on feet wobble as you sew, and this play in the foot position will affect the accuracy of the seams. This is especially true if the foot has a little guide built onto the right side of it. These guides aren't always an accurate ¼˝ to start with, and any movement while sewing will throw off your seam allowance just enough to cause problems.

- Check the **fabric position**. If you see a bit of fabric beyond the right side of the ¼˝ foot, you are taking too wide a seam. If you don't see the edge of the fabric, where are you looking to guide the fabric under the foot? Is it going through the machine straight?

Chapter 2: Quilting Fabric

Choosing Fabrics

BY ALEX ANDERSON

Quilting stores are found all over the world. It is in quilting stores that we can get the finest 100% cotton fabrics available. Different grades of cloth are used for the printed fabrics available to us. You want to use the best you can find. The less-expensive cottons are loosely woven with fewer threads per inch and will only cause you problems as they stretch and distort. Stay away from poly/cotton blends, which will shrink right before your eyes as you press the shapes.

As an avid fabric lover and collector, the thought of starting from scratch seems foreign to me. As I look back to my early days, I realize I did not really start to feel confident with fabric choices until after I had made several quilts. The fabric will dictate your quilt's mood or look. Each quilt in this book uses a different approach to fabric selection, which is briefly discussed at the onset of each project. Once you have decided what look you want, there are two vital rules to keep in mind.

- Always use light-, medium-, and dark-colored fabrics. Look how the second example below is composed only of mediums. It lacks the punch that the third example has. Medium fabrics are usually the most appealing, but force yourself to integrate both lights and darks. Using a combination of lights, mediums, and darks will make your quilt sparkle.

- Use printed fabrics that have variety in the character of the print. *Character of the print* refers to the design and scale of the print on the cloth. New quiltmakers often come to the craft with an image of what quilting prints should look like—that is, small calicos. However, when you use only one type of print, your quilt may look like it has the chicken pox. See how much more interesting the third example is than the first? This is because the third example not only has light, medium, and dark prints but also contains fabric with different characters of print, or visual texture. There are fabulous prints in delicious colors available to us. Never judge a fabric by how it looks on the bolt. We are not making clothing. Remember, when the fabric is cut up, it will look quite different.

Don't use fabrics with all the same scale of print.

Don't use all the same value (lightness and darkness) of fabrics.

Do use fabrics with a variety of values and scale of prints.

tip Try this trick: Take a 4″ square of cardboard and cut a 2″-square hole in the center. Position the cardboard over the fabric to see how the fabric will "read" when used in patchwork.

Be open to using fabrics that might make you feel uncomfortable. Remember, you aren't wearing the fabric; you are cutting it into little pieces and making a quilt. Experiment. That is how I grew to love and understand fabric relationships.

GRAIN OF THE FABRIC

When fabric is produced, threads are woven in two directions, creating a length and a width. This is called the straight of grain. If you cut diagonally across the grain (in triangle pieces), you are working on the bias. Bias edges must be sewn and pressed carefully, because they stretch easily. The long finished edges of the fabric are called the selvages. Always trim off the selvage edges—they cause distortion of the block and are difficult to hand quilt.

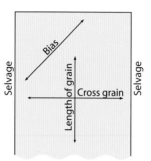

Grain of fabric

tip When prewashing your fabric, unfold it completely before you put it in the washing machine, so you don't get a permanent fade mark along the original fold.

PREPARING THE FABRIC

There are different schools of thought as to whether you should prewash your fabric. My philosophy is that you should, and here are three reasons.

• When the quilt is laundered, 100% cotton shrinks, causing puckers and distortion in the quilt.

• Darker dyes have been known to migrate to the lighter fabrics. This defines the expression "heartbreak."

• Fabric is treated with chemicals, and I don't think it is healthy to breathe or handle these chemicals over an extended period. I sometimes find myself wheezing when I decide to pass up prewashing.

tip Always prewash darks and lights separately.

If you are working with a dark piece of fabric (reds and purples are extremely suspect), test your fabric by cutting a 2″ square and putting it in boiling water. If any color bleeds, wash your fabric in Retayne, Synthrapol, or a half-and-half solution of white vinegar and water. Dry and retest the fabric. If it still runs, repeat the solution process. If the fabric continues to run, throw it away. It could ruin your quilt.

Fabric Vocabulary

BY ELIZABETH HARTMAN

Selvage is the finished edge of the fabric. The selvages of quilting fabrics are usually printed with the name of the fabric and designer and are often quite attractive by themselves. Some quilters like to save their selvages to use in other projects.

Fold refers to the center fold created when fabric is folded selvage to selvage, as it is on the bolt.

Grain refers to the way the threads in the weave of a woven fabric line up with the selvage. With cotton and linen fabrics, the grain is parallel and perpendicular to the selvage. Fabric cut along the grain is stable and ideal for patchwork piecing.

Bias means diagonal in relation to the grain. Fabric cut on the bias (for instance, fabric that has been cut into triangles) has a tendency to stretch along the bias edge and requires careful handling.

Width is the distance from selvage to selvage. In most cases this is about 42″–44″. (In order to account for a wide variety of fabrics, the projects in this book assume a 40″ width unless otherwise stated.)

Length is the distance from cut edge to cut edge, along the selvage. The length of the fabric is the length of the cut. For instance, a perfect 2-yard cut should be 72″ in length.

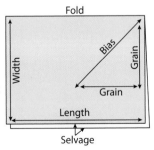

Right and wrong sides The right side of the fabric is the side you want showing in your finished project—usually the side with a pattern printed on it. The wrong side is, of course, the opposite side, which you don't want to show.

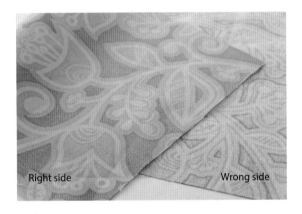

Right side   Wrong side

tip It can be difficult to identify the right and wrong sides of some fabrics, especially solids and batiks. In theory, you should choose one side and stick with it. In practice, it can be difficult to keep track of which side is which. Don't spend too much time fretting about the difference between seemingly identical right and wrong sides. If you can't tell the difference, it's unlikely to harm your project.

Choosing Fabrics Based on the Color Wheel

BY BECKY GOLDSMITH

Color wheels are pretty, and that's why we like looking at them. Beyond being pretty, however, a color wheel is a powerful tool that shows the relationships between colors. This is important because knowing how colors work together will help you use color better in your quilts.

Some people have spent their lives studying color theory. I am not one of them. I do have a degree in interior design, and what I learned in school has been valuable—but you do not need a college degree to be able to use a color wheel. I promise.

HOW THE COLOR WHEEL WORKS

It is easier to use a color wheel if you know why it is put together the way it is. The color wheels in this book are divided into twelve wedges that represent the twelve basic colors. There are more complex color wheels, with more colors and wedges, but for this book, a simple color wheel works best.

Besides being divided into wedges, the color wheel is also divided into five concentric rings. The colors are lighter in the rings toward the center and darker in the rings to the outside.

The True Colors

The middle ring on the color wheel is occupied by the *truest color*, or hue, in each wedge.

Primary Colors

Primary colors are the only colors on the wheel that are not made from combining other colors. They are positioned an equal distance apart, separating the wheel into thirds.

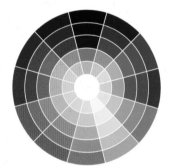

The color wheel

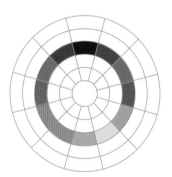

The truest colors occupy the middle ring.

Primary colors cannot be made from other colors.

Secondary Colors

Secondary colors are halfway between the primary colors and are made by mixing together the two nearest primary colors.

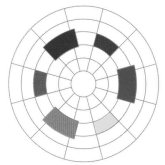

Secondary colors fall halfway between the primary colors.

Tertiary Colors

Tertiary means "third in order or level," and that is an apt description of these colors. *Tertiary colors* fall between adjacent primary and secondary colors and are a mix of the colors on either side.

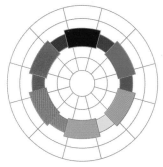

Tertiary colors fall between adjacent primary and secondary colors.

Now that you know how it works, the color wheel is pretty easy to decipher.

NEUTRALS

Neutral colors (white, gray, black, beige, brown) rarely show up on the color wheel. They are not associated with any specific color, although some neutrals do have undertones of one color or another.

Even though they are not "colorful," neutrals are very important to quilters. Colors shine against them, which is why you so often see neutrals used

Neutrals are not associated with any specific color.

as backgrounds. Solid neutrals, in particular, showcase the colors and fabrics that they are paired with. When neutrals are used by themselves, the resulting quilts can be calm—or exciting.

About Black-and-White Prints

When you buy black-and-white prints, it is because you want both black and white. However, you need to be aware that these prints can look gray in your quilt.

A black-and-white print with more white space is more likely to read as distinctly black and white. Prints that have small or thin black motifs set closely together, without much white space, can appear to be gray when viewed from a distance.

If you want your quilt to read truly black and white, use prints that have more open areas of white between the areas of black.

Black-and-white prints

COLOR TEMPERATURE

Warm colors range from yellow to red-violet. They have a reputation for being comfy, cozy, embracing colors.

Cool colors range from yellow-green to blue-violet. They might be considered calm, sophisticated, and less emotional.

You may have read that warm colors come forward in a composition and that cool colors recede. Sometimes that is true, and sometimes it isn't. To my eye, what determines a color's place on the visual plane depends on clarity, value, and the other colors in view.

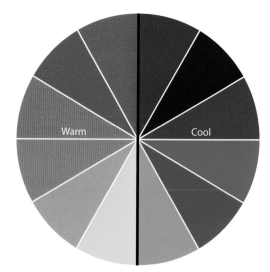

The color wheel can be divided into warm and cool colors.

Because this is a practical guide to color rather than a treatise on color theory, I can say that I rarely think about the temperature of a color. I know which colors make me happy, and those are the colors that I buy and use, regardless of their temperature.

MONOCHROMATIC COLOR SCHEMES

A *monochromatic color scheme* combines different values of only one color. This color scheme often has a calm demeanor. Working in monochrome is one way of learning how to manage differences in value without having to worry about combining different colors.

Many of the colors on the color wheel are easy to work with in monochrome. Greens, blues, purples, yellows, oranges—from the lightest pastel tints to

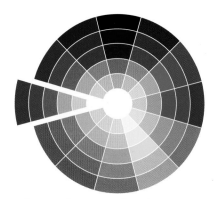

A monochromatic color scheme uses different values of only one color.

the darkest shades, each of these is still recognizably "that" color. The same is true for neutrals. From cream to dark brown, or from white through gray to black, the different values don't turn into some other color.

It is more difficult to build a red monochromatic color scheme. Red fabrics tend to lean toward either blue or orange. As blue-reds get lighter, they turn pink. As orange-reds get lighter, they turn light rosy orange. If you want a quilt that reads "red," pink and orange are not good choices.

COMPLEMENTARY COLOR SCHEMES

When you combine *complementary colors*, or colors that are directly across from each other on the color wheel, the result is often dynamic and full of energy. A good example is the combination of red and green. Think of all the times you have seen red and green together at Christmas. They always look great together.

You can use complementary colors in equal amounts in a composition—or use less of one color and more of the other. I used the same amounts of both blue and orange in my quilt *Opposites Attract* (see detail photo, at right). White separates the two complementary colors in this quilt, giving them space to breathe.

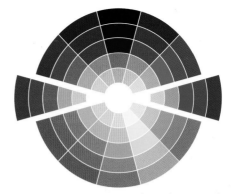

Complementary colors are those that are right across from each other on the color wheel.

Detail of *Opposites Attract* by Becky Goldsmith. Complementary colors orange and blue are a happy, vibrant combination.

SPLIT-COMPLEMENTARY COLOR SCHEMES

A *split-complementary color scheme* is made up of one color plus the colors on either side of its complement. In this example, red is the color that determines the other two colors.

I used the same, slightly expanded, split-complementary color scheme in *The Ground (As Seen from Above)* (see detail photo, below right). The quilt is predominantly yellow-green, with a mix of reds and some purples. Aqua blue, the third color in this color scheme, is used less, but it is still an important accent color.

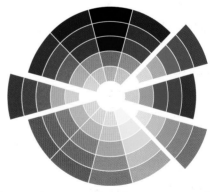

A split-complementary color scheme uses one color and the colors on either side of the color's complement.

Detail of *The Ground (As Seen from Above)* by Becky Goldsmith. Although this quilt is mostly green and red, little bits of aqua add an important spark to it.

TRIADIC COLOR SCHEMES

A *triadic color scheme* uses three colors that are an equal distance apart on the color wheel. If you superimposed an equilateral triangle over the color wheel, these colors would be at the points. This is a good color scheme to use when choosing the colors for a three-color quilt.

Square Play is a quilt made with the three primary colors (red, blue, and yellow) that make up a triadic color scheme. I chose these colors intentionally as a personal challenge, because when I imagine primary colors, I see crayons and clowns, and that is not usually the look I am going for in a quilt.

What worked for me was to make red the dominant color, with vibrant accents of blue and yellow. The finished quilt looks more like a red bandana than a box of crayons.

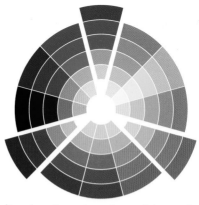

A triadic color scheme is made up of three colors that are an equal distance apart on the color wheel.

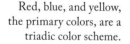

Red, blue, and yellow, the primary colors, are a triadic color scheme.

Square Play by Becky Goldsmith

ANALOGOUS COLOR SCHEMES

Analogous colors are those that are next to each other on the color wheel. They blend together happily.

A smooth transition from one color to another adds movement to a quilt. You can see this in *Picasso's Garden* (next page), where the blending of colors encourages you to look up and down the vines.

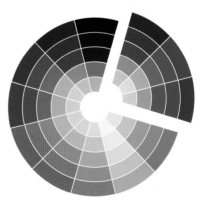

Analogous colors are next to each other on the color wheel.

Even when you choose colors that blend together, you do not have to use them right next to each other in the quilt. You can spread them around and still retain that beautiful, harmonious look.

Blues that blend into both purple and green are analogous colors that shine against the neutral browns in the background.

Picasso's Garden, 49″ × 57″, by Becky Goldsmith, 2007

RAINBOW COLOR SCHEMES

Rainbow color schemes are happy—your eyes are drawn to the movement and beauty of many colors blending together around the color wheel.

Rainbow fabrics do not have to be bright and bold; they can also be soft and light. Feel free to play with the intensity of the colors in your rainbow to suit the mood of your quilt. I had fun using a softer rainbow of colors in *Stairway to Heaven* (at right).

If you look at the colorful fabric in this quilt, you might notice that the colors in the prints are not necessarily soft. For instance, the reds in the red prints are dark and bright. What makes these fabrics seem lighter and softer is that there is so much white in each of the prints.

Stairway to Heaven by Becky Goldsmith

Value and Contrast in Fabric

BY BECKY GOLDSMITH

What could be more important than color? Color is the exciting, *look-at-me-NOW* attention-getter. However, as fantastic as color is, the contrast between colors and values is the most important thing in the design of your quilts. There are many kinds of contrast: contrast between values, colors, scales, and textures. You need to understand each of these kinds of contrast because you will use them all.

VALUE

Value refers to how light or dark a color is. Every color has a value; it will be light, medium, dark— or somewhere in between.

When light and dark values are placed next to each other, they are easy to tell apart. The line that is formed between them is very visible. This is *high contrast*.

When the contrast is high, it is easy to see the difference between the light and dark values.

When values that are similar to each other are placed together, they are harder to tell apart. The line between them blurs. This is *low contrast*.

When the contrast is low, it is harder to see differences between the similar values.

COLOR AND CONTRAST

When quilters talk about *contrast*, they are usually talking about the contrast between values: light versus dark. But contrast is not about value alone. Colors contrast as well. Simply stated, we can see differences between colors, even when the values are similar.

Colors that are farther apart on the color wheel are more obviously different from each other. This is especially true for complementary colors (page 27). Even when the colors are similar in value, it is usually not hard to tell one complementary color from another.

It is easy to see the difference between red and green, complementary colors, even though the values are similar.

It is harder to see the difference between colors that are similar in value and that lie close together on the color wheel, like analogous colors (page 28).

It is harder to see the difference between red and orange, analogous colors, which are similar in value.

The Nature of Fabric

BY BECKY GOLDSMITH

SOLIDS

Solid-color fabric is the most predictable kind. No matter how you cut it, the color remains the same in every piece.

Solids are very versatile. They can be used with other solids or combined with prints. Depending on how you use them, solids can be quiet and unobtrusive (imagine a white background), or they can take center stage.

Solid fabric is very versatile and can be used with other solids or with prints.

It's easy to think of solids as boring, but quilts made with only solid fabrics are wonderfully graphic, whether the quilt is traditional or modern in design.

TEXTURED SOLIDS

The Postimpressionist painter Van Gogh used textured brushstrokes to give his paintings energy. You can use textured solids in a similar way to add movement to the quieter areas of your quilt.

Textured solids look solid from a distance, and they too are very predictable. Only as you get closer do you see the details in the print. Tone-on-tone prints are the most common kind of textured solid, combining more than one value of the same color.

Tone-on-tone prints are active solids.

Single-color, mottled hand-dyes and batiks are another kind of textured solid. They have a fluid visual texture without a distinctive pattern. When you want more than a flat, solid color in your quilt, add some textured solids into the mix.

Single-color mottled hand-dyes and batiks have a more fluid visual texture.

PRINTS

All printed fabric has contrast between the colors and values *inside the print itself.* The contrast found in the print relates directly to how quiet or active the fabric appears to be.

Printed fabrics have repeating patterns across the width and length of the fabric. The *repeat* refers to the length of the pattern before it repeats itself again. The repetition of shapes and colors gives the print a cohesive appearance. The smaller the pattern and repeat, the easier it is to predict what the fabric will look like when it is cut up.

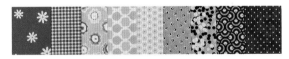

Small, regular prints are predictable.

A predictable print can be cut into big or small pieces and will look the same everywhere it shows up in the quilt. In pieced quilts, that is a very good thing.

CONVERSATION PRINTS

Conversation prints (sometimes called *novelty prints*) have identifiable "things" on them: bugs, teddy bears, Mount Rushmore.… Whatever the thing is, it is intended to be seen. Viewers notice these things—they might even have a conversation about them.

Conversation prints have identifiable, very visible "things" on them.

Conversation prints are perfect for children's quilts, where the intention is for the child to pick out different things in the fabric. These prints can be fun to use in seasonal quilts or in quilts with a theme.

I use conversation prints sparingly because I don't necessarily want the viewer to pick out a bug in the fabric before they see the design of the quilt itself. But these prints are fun to have in your stash.

BIG PRINTS

Big prints have an expansive feeling that is directly related to their large size. The motifs appear oversized next to other quilt fabric. The colors in these prints are often bold and bright and spaced widely apart. This print, Vivienne from Alexander Henry Fabrics, is a good example.

Big prints can be wild, with big designs and colors widely dispersed.

In appliqué, you can fussy cut shapes from different parts of the print. In piecing, you can fussy cut a fabric, but generally you begin by cutting strips. Strips and other small shapes cut from a large-print fabric are different enough that they could have come from four different fabrics. In a quilt pattern that requires regular color placement, that can be either a problem—or a virtue.

It's hard to tell that these squares came from the same piece of fabric.

The colors in a big print look good together; they don't clash. Different colors may dominate the various shapes cut from a big print, but these shapes will be color coordinated. If you set them against a common background, the results can be exciting.

Needle in a Haystack is a fun, two-fabric quilt. I would have had to work a lot harder to get the same effect from individual red, blue, and yellow fabrics.

tip Try Them—You'll Like Them

Big prints feel open and expansive, even when they are cut into small pieces. They add a particular kind of movement to a quilt. The scale of a big print especially stands out when combined with smaller-scale prints or solids. I would encourage you to keep some in your stash. It will be even better if you remember to use them.

Needle in a Haystack, 36″ × 36″, by Becky Goldsmith, 2014

Strips cut from the big print shine against a white background.

Chapter 3: Piecing

Rotary Cutting Basics

BY ELIZABETH HARTMAN

Rotary cutting should, in general, be done from a standing position. The vantage point gained by standing and the additional pressure you'll be able to put on the ruler will make for more accurate cutting. If possible, use your rotary cutter on a table that you can walk all the way around. This will minimize the number of times you have to move the fabric you're cutting.

All fabric should be free from wrinkles prior to cutting. This is essential to accurate cutting, so take the time to press your fabric before you work with it.

tip Safety First!

Before we start with cutting, let's talk about safety. Rotary cutter blades are very sharp and can cut you as easily as they cut fabric. Most cutters have a button to lock the position of the blade, and it's a good idea to get in the habit of using it. As you cut, keep all your fingers on the hand that's not holding the cutter on top of the ruler and out of the path of the cutter.

> **NOTE** *These instructions are written for right-handed people, and the photos show a right-handed person cutting. If you're left-handed, you'll want to do the opposite of what is described here, including moving the rotary cutter blade to the opposite side of the cutter.*

Unless otherwise noted in the directions, the ruler should always be lined up with the grain of the fabric. Hold it firmly in place with your left hand, keeping all your fingers on top of the ruler and out of the path of the cutter.

Prepare to cut by lining up the blade with the right edge of the ruler. Use even pressure to run the cutter along the edge of the ruler, making a clean cut through the fabric. As you cut, keep your fingers clear of the blade.

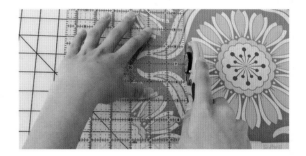

Change your rotary cutter blade regularly. Dull or nicked blades make accurate cutting more difficult and can cause ugly little pulls in the fabric. If it takes more than one pass with the cutter to get though the fabric, it's time to change the blade.

The first cuts you make from your fabric will usually be strips cut along the width or the length of the fabric. In most cases these strips are then cut into smaller pieces.

Cutting along the width (selvage to selvage) is easier and is how most pieces are cut. Cutting along the length (cut edge to cut edge) of the fabric is used to make longer sashing or border strips or backing pieces.

CUTTING ALONG THE WIDTH OF THE FABRIC

1. Fold the fabric selvage to selvage and place it on the cutting mat with the folded edge nearest you.

2. Lay a 6″ × 24″ ruler on top of the fabric. Match a horizontal line on the ruler to the fold and slide the ruler near the cut edge on the right side of the fabric.

3. Cut off a small strip of fabric along the right side of the ruler, creating a straight edge at a right angle to the fold. This is called "squaring up" the fabric.

4. Move to the opposite side of the table (or, if you cannot, carefully turn your rotary cutting mat around). Now the straight edge you just cut is on the left side of the fabric, and the folded edge away from you.

5. Use the lines on the ruler to measure the width of the strip you want to cut and, again, cut along the right side of the ruler. Continue making cuts, moving from left to right across the fabric.

CUTTING ALONG THE LENGTH OF THE FABRIC

Since fabric is usually about 42″–44″ wide, strips longer than this need to be cut along the length of the fabric (parallel to the selvage edge). To make an accurate cut, you'll first need to refold the fabric to a size that will fit on your mat.

Instead of folding the fabric along the existing fold, fold it in the opposite direction, bringing the cut edges together and matching the selvages along one side. Fold the fabric once or twice more, continuing to keep the selvages along one side

lined up, until you can easily lay the fabric on your cutting mat.

You may need to let one end of the fabric hang off the end of the table. Just be careful not to let its weight pull the nicely folded edge out of alignment. You may need to set a book or something else heavy on the folded fabric, out of the way of your cutting tools.

Trim away the selvage to square the edge and use this as the straight edge to cut the pattern pieces. You'll be cutting through more layers than you

would if you were cutting along the width, so be careful and realign the edge of the fabric as necessary.

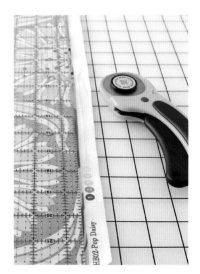

What if my ruler isn't wide enough?

Some of the patterns require larger pieces than you'll be able to cut with a 6″ × 24″ ruler alone. In those cases, use a 12½″ square ruler to add extra width. When you do this, always keep the 6″ × 24″ ruler on the right edge of the square ruler and cut along the narrow ruler's 24″ edge.

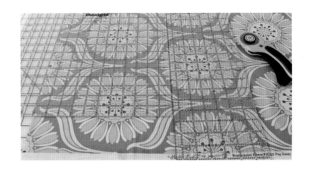

FUSSY CUTTING

Fussy cutting is the common term for cutting a print fabric in such a way as to center or otherwise highlight a particular part of the print.

Cut a piece of translucent template plastic (available at most quilt or craft shops) in the size of the piece you need and move it around the surface of the fabric until you find the part you want to highlight. Keep in mind that when you stitch the piece, you'll lose ¼″ on each side to the seam allowance.

Trace around the outside of the template with a disappearing-ink marker and use the marked lines to cut out the piece with either scissors or a ruler and rotary cutter.

Because you're using only certain parts of the print, fussy cutting takes up quite a bit more fabric than standard rotary cutting. How much more depends on the print, but, in general, I recommend buying twice as much of any fabric that you plan to fussy cut.

Patchwork Piecing Basics

BY ELIZABETH HARTMAN

In order to achieve sharp, precise piecing with a sewing machine, it's important to remember that every step of the process matters. The accuracy of your seam allowances, the way you press the seams, and whether or not you square up your blocks are all-important to duplicating this look.

However, there is absolutely no reason you can't take a more relaxed approach. If you prefer a wonky look or just aren't too concerned about having seams match up exactly, go for it!

HAND PIECING

BY THE EDITORS AT C&T PUBLISHING

Hand piecing together a quilt is not hard, but it can be time consuming! Hand piecing is really just using a running stitch to join together the patchwork pieces. While it may be slower than machine stitching, there are many advantages to hand piecing.

Pros

- It's portable. It's wonderful to have projects that can be worked on "on the go." Just keep a little baggie of cut and marked pieces, a spool of thread, a needle, and thread snips in your purse or backpack, and you're set for long lines, car rides, and sports practices.

- It's relaxing. You can stitch on the couch while watching (and listening) to the television or on the front porch with a nice spring breeze.

- It's simple and inexpensive. No need to purchase a machine or learn complicated techniques.

- It's precise. Because the sewing machine isn't moving you through the work quickly, you can take the time to easily match points.

Supplies

- Pencil or water-erasable pen

- Cotton thread

- Sharps or milliners needles (There is no right or wrong needle for hand piecing. Just use whatever feels right to you.)

- Fabric and your pattern (of course!)

Steps for Traditional Hand Piecing

1. Mark the sewing lines.

2. Cut out the shapes, leaving an approximate ¼″ seam allowance.

3. Pin the pieces right sides together, aligning the stitching lines.

4. Knot your thread if desired. (Alternatively, leave a ¼″ tail and backstitch a few stitches.)

5. Start the stitching line by putting the needle through the marked corner on the top piece and out the corner on the bottom piece.

6. Take one stitch and then backstitch to secure it.

7. Use a running stitch to complete the seam.

8. At the end, backstitch and tie a knot.

9. Finger-press the seam. (Press the seams with an iron when your block is constructed.)

STITCH QUALITY

Using a ¼˝ seam foot (page 8), sew the patchwork pieces together using a small to medium stitch length. I prefer the 2 to 3 setting on my machine, which appears to be about 12 stitches per inch. Before you start sewing on your quilt fabric, test your machine's stitch on scrap fabric and make adjustments if necessary.

In general, if the top of your project looks puckered and the bobbin thread appears to be pulled in a straight line, the thread tension is too tight. If the top thread and bobbin thread are loopy, the thread tension may be too loose. I recommend consulting your machine's manual when making tension adjustments.

Before You Adjust the Tension …

If my stitch is bad, the first thing I do is to change my needle. Always. Even if I haven't been using that needle for very long. (Sometimes even a brand-new needle can create poor-quality stitches.) Needles do a lot of work, and even the smallest nick can affect their performance.

Another thing to check is the thread. I cannot stress enough the importance of using quality thread. Switching to a better thread can make a huge difference in stitch quality.

Last but not least, check the bobbin. Take out the bobbin casing and make sure there are no loose threads caught around it. Make sure the bobbin is wound properly and then place it back in the machine.

PINNING

I pin pretty much everything before I sew it, inserting pins through all the layers on both sides of each seam allowance. If there's a large space between seam allowances, I place a pin or two there as well.

Keep a pincushion next to your machine and remove pins as you sew. All this pinning may seem tedious, but it will lead to accuracy.

tip When sewing together a solid piece of fabric (for instance, a piece of sashing) and a pieced block, always keep the pieced block on top. This will help you keep an eye on the block's seam allowances and ensure that they don't get pulled askew by your machine's feed dogs.

CHAIN PIECING

A great way to save both time and thread, chain piecing is sort of like running a mini assembly line. Gather similar pairs of pieces and run them through your machine one after the other without stopping to clip the threads between pieces. When you're done, clip the threads between each set and press as usual.

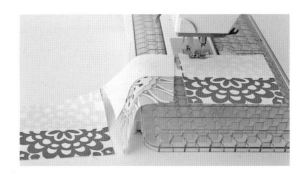

PRESSING SEAMS

I press my seams open. It takes a bit more effort than pressing to the side, as many quilters do, but I think the results are worth it. Your finished blocks will be more precise, will lie flatter, and will be easier to machine quilt in an allover pattern. The even distribution of the seam allowances should also ensure that the quilt wears more evenly.

Lay your work right side down on the pressing surface and use your index finger to press open the seam. Follow this by running the point of your iron down the seam. Then place the entire iron over the seam and press firmly,

adding a little burst of steam. Flip the work over and gently iron the front (right) side.

For long seams, I usually lay my work faceup on the pressing surface, press to one side, and then flip the project over to press the seam open.

Some quilters believe that pressing seams open will have a negative impact on the structural integrity of the quilt. I have never found this to be true. As long as you're using a good stitch and good materials, a quilt made with pressed-open seams should be perfectly sturdy.

Pressing to the side is easier, and many quilters like it for this reason. If you're a devoted side presser, I may not be able to change your mind. I just encourage you to give open pressing a try.

Blocks to Get You Started

BY THE EDITORS AT C&T PUBLISHING

Practice your piecing with a gallery of 25 quilt blocks (pages 39–46). The easy-to-use cutting charts will guide you to make blocks in five different sizes by piecing squares, triangles, strips, and more. Refer to the sample diagram and block (below) and the chart key (next page) for how to use the block charts.

HOW TO USE THE BLOCK CHARTS

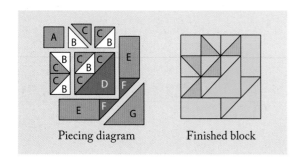

Piecing diagram   Finished block

Which piece	How many to cut of each piece/fabric	How many you need of each piece/fabric	Blocks				
For	Cut	Need	4″	6″	8″	10″	12″
A	1	1	1½	2	2½	3	3½
B	3	5	1⅞	2⅜	2⅞	3⅜	3⅞
C	4	7	1⅞	2⅜	2⅞	3⅜	3⅞
D	1	1	2⅞	3⅞	4⅞	5⅞	6⅞
E	2	2	1½ × 2½	2 × 3½	2½ × 4½	3 × 5½	3½ × 6½
F	1	2	1⅞	2⅜	2⅞	3⅜	3⅞
G	1	1	2⅞	3⅞	4⅞	5⅞	6⅞

Chart Key

WOF = width of fabric

LOFQ = length of fat quarter

Single dimension =

Cut diagonally =

Width × length dimension =

Cut diagonally, twice =

Air Castle

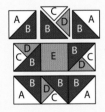
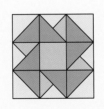

For	Cut	Need	3″	6″	9″	12″	15″
A	2	4	1⅞	2⅞	3⅞	4⅞	5⅞
B	4	8	1⅞	2⅞	3⅞	4⅞	5⅞
C	1	4	2¼	3¼	4¼	5¼	6¼
D	1	4	2¼	3¼	4¼	5¼	6¼
E	1	1	1½	2½	3½	4½	5½

Arkansas Crossroads

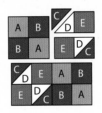
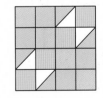

For	Cut	Need	4″	6″	8″	10	12″
A	4	4	1½	2	2½	3	3½
B	4	4	1½	2	2½	3	3½
C	2	4	1⅞	2⅜	2⅞	3⅜	3⅞
D	2	4	1⅞	2⅜	2⅞	3⅜	3⅞
E	4	4	1½	2	2½	3	3½

Aztec Jewel

 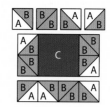

For	Cut	Need	3″	6″	9″	12″	15″
A	4 ☐	4 ◨	1	1½	2	2½	3
B	8 ☐	16 ◹	1⅜	1⅞	2⅜	2⅞	3⅜
C	4 ◨	8 ◸	1⅜	1⅞	2⅜	2⅞	3⅜
D	1 ■	4 ⊠	2¼	3¼	4¼	5¼	6¼
E	2 ☐	4 ◹	1⅞	2⅞	3⅞	4⅞	5⅞
F	1 ◨	4 ⊠	2¼	3¼	4¼	5¼	6¼
G	1 ■	1 ■	1½	2½	3½	4½	5½

Balkan Puzzle

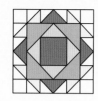

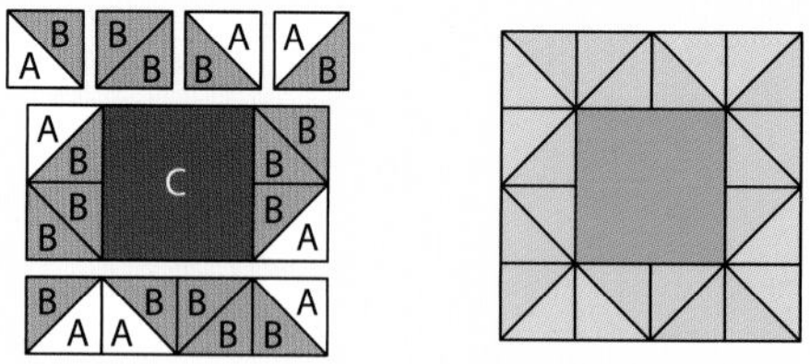

For	Cut	Need	4″	6″	8″	10″	12″
A	4 ☐	8 ◹	1⅞	2⅜	2⅞	3⅜	3⅞
B	8 ◨	16 ◹	1⅞	2⅜	2⅞	3⅜	3⅞
C	1 ■	1 ■	2½	3½	4½	5½	6½

Basket—Cake Stand Basket

For	Cut	Need	4″	6″	8″	10″	12″
A	1 ☐	1 ☐	1½	2	2½	3	3½
B	3 ■	6 ◹	1⅞	2⅜	2⅞	3⅜	3⅞
C	2 ☐	4 ◹	1⅞	2⅜	2⅞	3⅜	3⅞
D	1 ◨	1 ◹	2⅞	3⅞	4⅞	5⅞	6⅞
E	1 ■	1 ◹	2⅞	3⅞	4⅞	5⅞	6⅞
F	2 ▭	2 ▭	1½ × 2½	2 × 3½	2½ × 4½	3 × 5½	3½ × 6½
G	1 ☐	1 ◹	2⅞	3⅞	4⅞	5⅞	6⅞

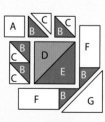

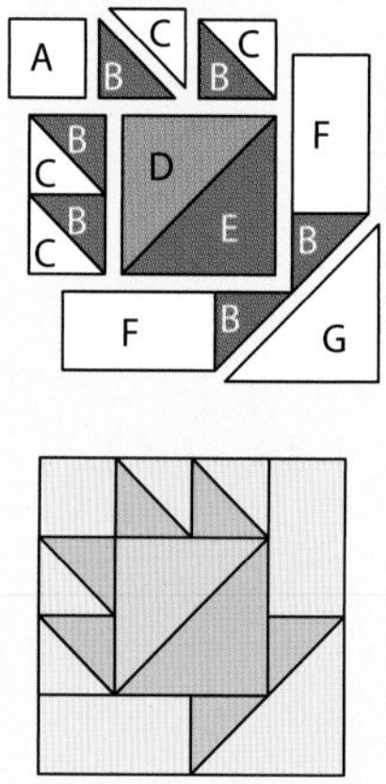

Basket—Cherry Basket

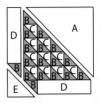

For	Cut	Need	3″	6″	9″	12″	15″
A	1 ☐	1 ◺	3⅜	5⅞	8⅜	10⅞	13⅜
B	9 ■	17 ◣	1⅜	1⅞	2⅜	2⅞	3⅜
C	5 ☐	10 ◺	1⅜	1⅞	2⅜	2⅞	3⅜
D	2 ▭	2 ▭	1 × 2½	1½ × 4½	2 × 6½	2½ × 8½	3 × 10½
E	1 ☐	1 ◺	1⅞	2⅞	3⅞	4⅞	5⅞

Bias strips cut ½″–1½″ wide can be used for the handle.

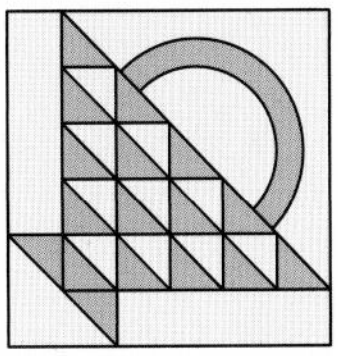

Basket—Flower Basket

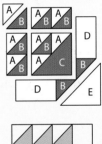

For	Cut	Need	4″	6″	8″	10″	12″
A	4 ☐	8 ◺	1⅞	2⅜	2⅞	3⅜	3⅞
B	4 ■	8 ◣	1⅞	2⅜	2⅞	3⅜	3⅞
C	1 ■	1 ◣	2⅞	3⅞	4⅞	5⅞	6⅞
D	2 ▭	2 ▭	1½ × 2½	2 × 3½	2½ × 4½	3 × 5½	3½ × 6½
E	1 ☐	1 ◺	2⅞	3⅞	4⅞	5⅞	6⅞

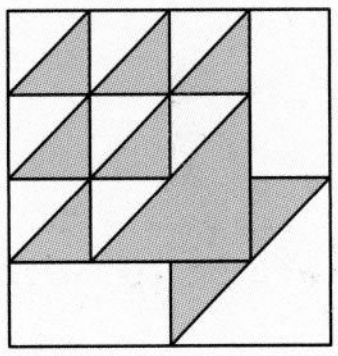

Basket—Star Basket

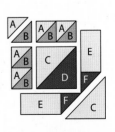

For	Cut	Need	4″	6″	8″	10″	12″
A	1 ☐	1 ☐	1½	2	2½	3	3½
B	1 ☐	2 ⊠	3¼	4¼	5¼	6¼	7¼
C	2 ▥	4 ◺	1⅞	2⅜	2⅞	3⅜	3⅞
D	1 ▥	1 ◺	2⅞	3⅞	4⅞	5⅞	6⅞
E	1 ■	1 ◣	2⅞	3⅞	4⅞	5⅞	6⅞
F	2 ▭	2 ▭	1½ × 2½	2 × 3½	2½ × 4½	3 × 5½	3½ × 6½
G	1 ■	2 ◣	1⅞	2⅜	2⅞	3⅜	3⅞
H	1 ☐	1 ◺	2⅞	3⅞	4⅞	5⅞	6⅞

Bow Tie

For	Cut	Need	4″	6″	8″	10″	12″
A	2 ☐	2 ☐	2½	3½	4½	5½	6½
B	2 ▨	2 ▨	2½	3½	4½	5½	6½
C	2 ▨	2 ▨	1½	2	2½	3	3½

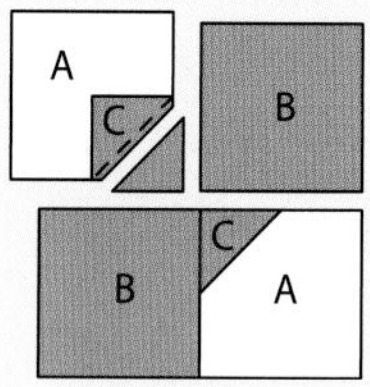

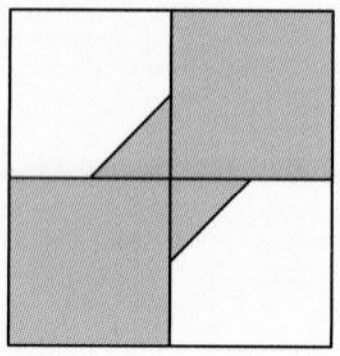

Buttercup

For	Cut	Need	3″	6″	9″	12″	15″
A	1 ▭	1 ▭	1 × 1½	1½ × 2½	2 × 3½	2½ × 4½	3 × 5½
B	1 ☐	1 ☐	1	1½	2	2½	3
C	1 ▨	1 ▨	1	1½	2	2½	3
D	1 ▨	2 ◪	1⅞	2⅞	3⅞	4⅞	5⅞
E	2 ☐	4 ◩	1⅞	2⅞	3⅞	4⅞	5⅞
F	3 ☐	3 ☐	1½	2½	3½	4½	5½
G	1 ▨	1 ▨	1½	2½	3½	4½	5½
H	1 ▨	2 ◪	1⅞	2⅞	3⅞	4⅞	5⅞

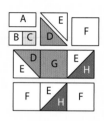

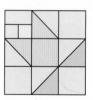

Cat's Cradle

For	Cut	Need	3″	6″	9″	12″	15″
A	2 ☐	2 ☐	1½	2½	3½	4½	5½
B	9 ▨	18 ◪	1⅜	1⅞	2⅜	2⅞	3⅜
C	3 ☐	6 ◪	1⅜	1⅞	2⅜	2⅞	3⅜
D	3 ☐	6 ◪	1⅞	2⅞	3⅞	4⅞	5⅞
E	1 ▨	1 ▨	1½	2½	3½	4½	5½

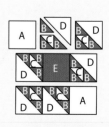

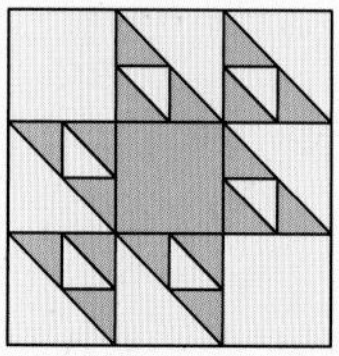

Combination Star

For	Cut	Need	3″	6″	9″	12″	15″
A	5 ■	5 ■	1¼	2	2⅝	3⅜	4
B	10 □	20 ◿	1⅜	1⅞	2⅜	2⅞	3⅜
C	2 ■	8 ⊠	2¼	3¼	4¼	5¼	6¼
D	2 □	8 ⊠	2¼	3¼	4¼	5¼	6¼

Country Farm

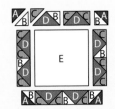 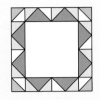

For	Cut	Need	3″	6″	9″	12″	15″
A	2 ■	4 ◿	1⅜	1⅞	2⅜	2⅞	3⅜
B	4 □	8 ◿	1⅜	1⅞	2⅜	2⅞	3⅜
C	6 ■	12 ◿	1⅜	1⅞	2⅜	2⅞	3⅜
D	2 ■	8 ⊠	2¼	3¼	4¼	5¼	6¼
E	1 □	1 □	2½	4½	6½	8½	10½

Cross Variation

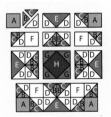 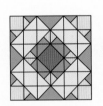

For	Cut	Need	6″	9″	12″	15″	18″
A	4 ■	4 ■	1½	2	2½	3	3½
B	4 ■	16 ⊠	2¼	2¾	3¼	3¾	4¼
C	4 ■	16 ⊠	2¼	2¾	3¼	3¾	4¼
D	12 □	24 ◿	1⅞	2⅜	2⅞	3⅜	3⅞
E	1 ■	4 ⊠	3¼	4¼	5¼	6¼	7¼
F	4 □	4 □	1½	2	2½	3	3½
G	2 ■	4 ◿	1⅞	2⅜	2⅞	3⅜	3⅞
H	1 ■	1 ■	2	2⅝	3⅜	4	4¾

Diamond Star

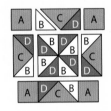

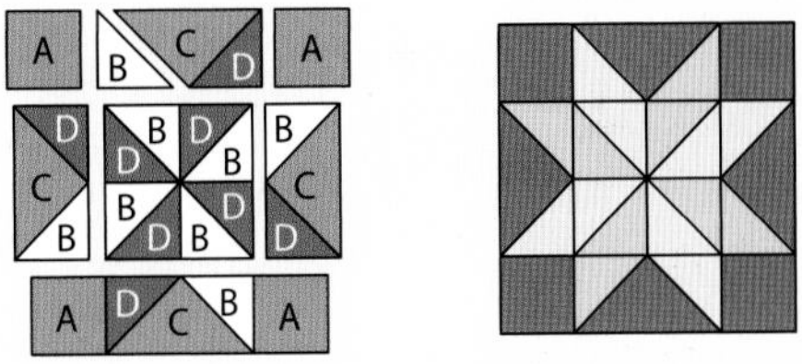

For	Cut	Need	4″	6″	8″	10″	12″
A	4 ■	4 ■	1½	2	2½	3	3½
B	4 □	8 ◿	1⅞	2⅜	2⅞	3⅜	3⅞
C	1 ■	4 ⊠	3¼	4¼	5¼	6¼	7¼
D	4 ■	8 ◿	1⅞	2⅜	2⅞	3⅜	3⅞

Double X

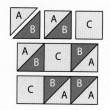 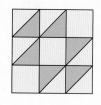

For	Cut	Need	3″	6″	9″	12″	15″
A	3 ☐	6 ◨	1⅞	2⅞	3⅞	4⅞	5⅞
B	3 ◼	6 ◪	1⅞	2⅞	3⅞	4⅞	5⅞
C	3 ☐	3 ☐	1½	2½	3½	4½	5½

Dutch Rose

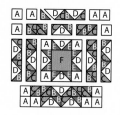 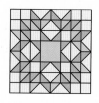

For	Cut	Need	6″	8″	10″	12″	14″
A	16 ☐	16 ☐	1¼	1½	1¾	2	2¼
B	12 ◼	24 ◪	1⅝	1⅞	2⅛	2⅜	2⅝
C	12 ◻	24 ◪	1⅝	1⅞	2⅛	2⅜	2⅝
D	4 ☐	16 ⊠	2¾	3¼	3¾	4¼	4¾
E	4 ◼	8 ◪	1⅝	1⅞	2⅛	2⅜	2⅝
F	1 ◻	1 ◻	2	2½	3	3½	4

Flying Geese

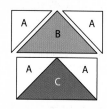

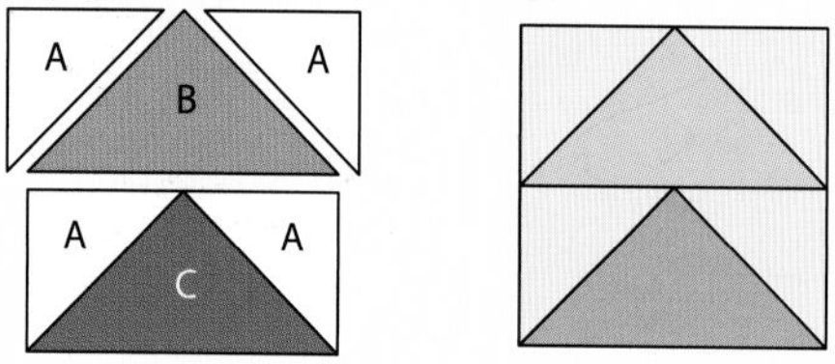

For	Cut	Need	4″	6″	8″	10″	12″
A	2 ☐	4 ◨	2⅞	3⅞	4⅞	5⅞	6⅞
B	1 ◻	1 ⊠	5¼	7¼	9¼	11¼	13¼
C	1 ◼	1 ⊠	5¼	7¼	9¼	11¼	13¼

Fox and Geese

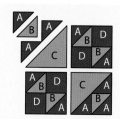 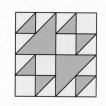

For	Cut	Need	4″	6″	8″	10″	12″
A	5 ◻	10 ◪	1⅞	2⅜	2⅞	3⅜	3⅞
B	3 ◼	6 ◪	1⅞	2⅜	2⅞	3⅜	3⅞
C	1 ◼	2 ◪	2⅞	3⅞	4⅞	5⅞	6⅞
D	4 ◻	4 ◻	1½	2	2½	3	3½

Garden Path

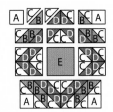

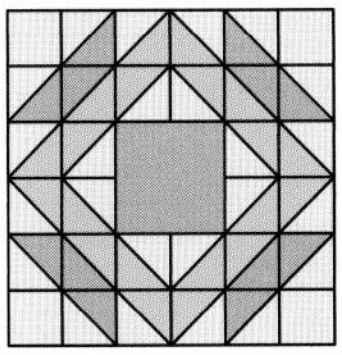

For	Cut	Need	3″	6″	9″	12″	15″
A	4 ☐	4 ☐	1	1½	2	2½	3
B	6 ◱	12 ◪	1⅜	1⅞	2⅜	2⅞	3⅜
C	12 ☐	24 ◪	1⅜	1⅞	2⅜	2⅞	3⅜
D	10 ◪	20 ◪	1⅜	1⅞	2⅜	2⅞	3⅜
E	1 ◱	1 ◱	1½	2½	3½	4½	5½

Grandmother's Choice

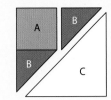

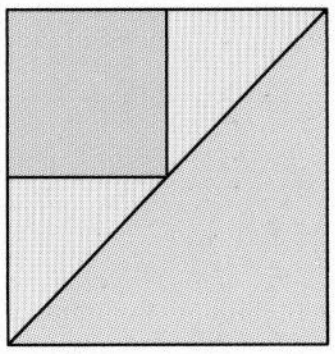

For	Cut	Need	4″	6″	8″	10″	12″
A	1 ◱	1 ◱	2½	3½	4½	5½	6½
B	1 ◼	2 ◪	2⅞	3⅞	4⅞	5⅞	6⅞
C	1 ☐	1 ◪	4⅞	6⅞	8⅞	10⅞	12⅞

Heart

For	Cut	Need	4″	6″	8″	10″	12″
A	2 ☐	4 ◪	1⅞	2⅜	2⅞	3⅜	3⅞
B	1 ◼	2 ⊠	3¼	4¼	5¼	6¼	7¼
C	2 ▬	2 ▬	1½ × 2½	2 × 3½	2½ × 4½	3 × 5½	3½ × 6½
D	1 ☐	2 ◪	2⅞	3⅞	4⅞	5⅞	6⅞
E	1 ◼	2 ◪	2⅞	3⅞	4⅞	5⅞	6⅞

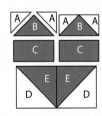

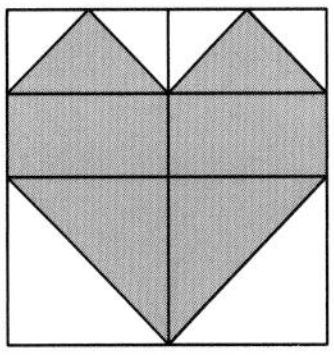

Home Grown

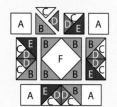

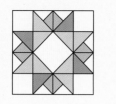

For	Cut	Need	6″	8″	10″	12″	14″
A	4 □	4 □	2	2½	3	3½	4
B	4 ■	8 ⧄	2⅜	2⅞	3⅜	3⅞	4⅜
C	2 □	8 ⊠	2¾	3¼	3¾	4¼	4¾
D	2 ■	8 ⊠	2¾	3¼	3¾	4¼	4¾
E	2 ■	4 ⧄	2⅜	2⅞	3⅜	3⅞	4⅜
F	1 □	1 □	2⅝	3⅜	4	4¾	5½

Indian Star

For	Cut	Need	4″	6″	8″	10″	12″
A	6 ■	6 ■	1½	2	2½	3	3½
B	4 ■	8 ⧄	1⅞	2⅜	2⅞	3⅜	3⅞
C	4 □	8 ⧄	1⅞	2⅜	2⅞	3⅜	3⅞
D	2 □	2 □	1½	2	2½	3	3½

Homeward Bound

For	Cut	Need	4″	6″	8″	10″	12″
A	2 □	4 ⧄	2⅞	3⅞	4⅞	5⅞	6⅞
B	2 ■	4 ⧄	2⅞	3⅞	4⅞	5⅞	6⅞

Piecing Tips

BY THE EDITORS AT C&T PUBLISHING

FIGURING FABRIC FOR A QUILT

To determine how much of each fabric you'll need for the blocks in a quilt:

1. Choose a block (or blocks) you want to use.

2. Determine how many blocks you'll need to create a quilt in the desired size.

3. Figure how many of each size square and rectangle you'll need from each fabric, and refer to Yardage for Squares (page 164) and Yardage for Rectangles (page 165).

It's as easy as that!

EASY-CUT 45° ANGLES

Place the 45° line of the rotary ruler on the edge of the fabric and trim as shown. Rotate the ruler and repeat if necessary.

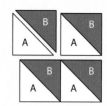

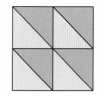

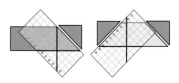

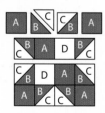

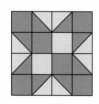

SEWING HALF-SQUARE TRIANGLES

1. With right sides together, pair 2 squares. Lightly draw a diagonal line from one corner to the opposite corner on the wrong sides of one square.

Draw line.

2. Sew a scant ¼˝ seam on each side of the line.

Sew.

3. Cut on the drawn line.

4. Press, and then trim off the dog-ears.

SEWING SQUARES TO SQUARES

1. Place the squares right sides together.

2. Sew diagonally from corner to corner.

3. Trim and press.

Stitching line   Discard triangles.

Trim ¼˝ from stitching line.

SEAM ALLOWANCES

Use a ¼˝-wide seam allowance throughout.

SEWING PARTIAL SEAMS

1. Place the first pieced unit or strip on one edge of the center square. Beginning ½˝ in from the edge of the center square, stitch along the top edge.

Start here.

2. Working clockwise around the center square, stitch the second pieced unit/strip. Repeat for the remaining 2 pieced units/strips.

3. Finish stitching the first pieced unit/strip. Press.

Red = Completed stitches.

CORNER ALIGNMENT FOR PIECING SHAPES

BY ALEX ANDERSON

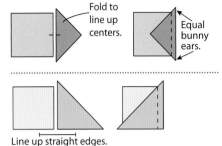

Fold to line up centers.   Equal bunny ears.

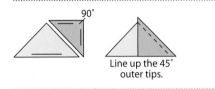

Line up straight edges.

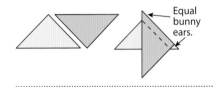

90°   Line up the 45° outer tips.

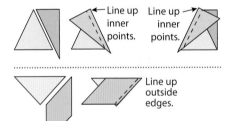

Equal bunny ears.

Line up inner points.   Line up inner points.

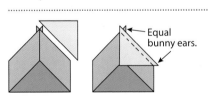

Line up outside edges.

Equal bunny ears.

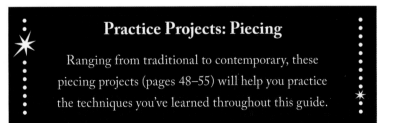

Practice Projects: Piecing

Ranging from traditional to contemporary, these piecing projects (pages 48–55) will help you practice the techniques you've learned throughout this guide.

Mod Pillow

BY SHERRI MCCONNELL

FINISHED BLOCK: 3″ × 3″

FINISHED PILLOW: 18″ × 18″

The mixture of solids and modern prints in this pillow showcases all the fabrics beautifully. I love the contrast between the solid white and solid gray, and the use of the white for the pillow binding really sets everything off.

Pieced by Sherri McConnell and quilted by Gail Begay

Fabric collections: Love by Amy Butler; Bella Solids by Moda

MATERIALS

ASSORTED PRINTS: ¼ yard total

WHITE: ⅜ yard

GRAY SOLID: ⅛ yard

BORDER: ¼ yard

PILLOW BACK: ⅝ yard

BINDING: ¼ yard

BATTING: 22″ × 22″

MUSLIN: 22″ × 22″

PILLOW FORM: 18″ × 18″

CUTTING

ASSORTED PRINTS: Cut 5 squares 4½″ × 4½″ for Hourglass blocks.

WHITE:

• Cut 5 squares 4½″ × 4½″ for Hourglass blocks.

• Cut 2 strips 2″ × width of fabric; subcut into 2 strips 2″ × 11½″ and 2 strips 2″ × 14½″ for middle borders.

GRAY: Cut 2 strips 1½″ × width of fabric; subcut into 2 strips 1½″ × 9½″ and 2 strips 1½″ × 11½″ for inner borders.

BORDER: Cut 2 strips 2½″ × width of fabric; subcut into 2 strips 2½″ × 14½″ and 2 strips 2½″ × 18½″ for outer borders.

PILLOW BACK: Cut 1 square 18½″ × 18½″ and 1 rectangle 18½″ × 16″.

BINDING: Cut 3 strips 2¼″ × width of fabric.

Block Assembly

Seam allowances are ¼˝ unless otherwise noted.

1. Draw a diagonal line from corner to corner on the wrong side of the white 4½˝ × 4½˝ squares.

2. Place a white 4½˝ × 4½˝ square right sides together with a print 4½˝ × 4½˝ square and make half-square triangles. Refer to Sewing Half-Square Triangles (page 47). Make 10.

Make 10.

3. Draw a diagonal line from corner to

corner, perpendicular to the seam on the wrong side of a half-square triangle unit. Place it right sides together with a matching half-square triangle unit, with light and dark fabrics facing each other and nesting the seams together. Stitch a scant ¼˝ on each side of the drawn line. Cut the squares apart on the drawn line; press the seam allowances to one side. Trim these 2 Hourglass blocks to 3½˝ × 3½˝. Make 10. (You need 9; you'll have 1 extra.)

4. Arrange 9 Hourglass blocks into 3 rows of 3 blocks each. Rotate every other block 90° (see the pillow top assembly diagram). Sew the blocks into rows and press. Sew the rows together; press.

5. Sew the 1½˝ × 9½˝ gray inner border strips to the left and right sides of the pillow center. Press the seams toward the gray fabric. Sew the 1½˝ × 11½˝ gray inner border strips to the top and bottom. Press the seams toward the gray fabric.

6. Sew the 2˝ × 11½˝ white middle border strips to the left and right sides of the pillow top. Press the seams toward the white fabric. Sew the 2˝ × 14½˝ white middle border strips to the top and bottom. Press the seams toward the white fabric.

7. Sew the 2½˝ × 14½˝ print outer border strips to the left and right sides of the pillow top. Press the seams toward the border fabric. Sew the 2½˝ × 18½˝ print outer border strips to the top and bottom. Press the seams toward the border fabric.

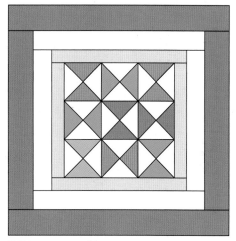
Pillow top assembly

Pillow Assembly

1. Place the 22˝ × 22˝ square of batting on the muslin. Center the pillow top on the batting and quilt as desired. Gail machine quilted an allover feather pattern on the pillow top.

2. Trim the batting even with the edges of the pillow top.

3. Make the pillow back by folding in and pressing ¼˝ on one 18½˝ edge of each pillow back section. Fold again, press, and sew along the pressed edge to create a finished outside edge.

4. Press the hemmed edges in 2˝, with wrong sides of the fabric together.

5. To complete the pillow, follow the instructions in Pillow Sham, Finish the Pillow, Steps 3 and 4 (page 152).

Basket Weave

BY ALISSA HAIGHT CARLTON

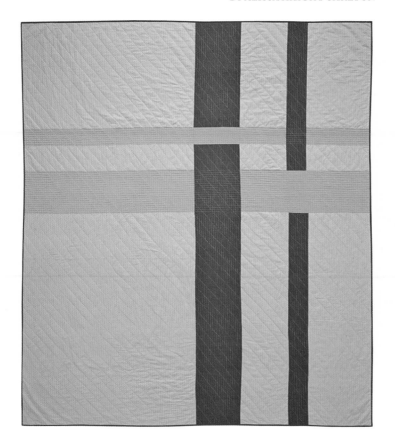

FINISHED QUILT: 90″ × 95″

This fun plaid quilt is big enough for a queen-size bed. Making a large bed quilt is definitely more time consuming than making a smaller quilt, but when it is this quick to piece, it's a very manageable task to take on. Why not make this quilt in darker colors for a simple masculine design that your favorite guy is certain to love?

MATERIALS

Based on 42″ fabric width.

FABRIC A (AQUA): 4⅝ yards for background

FABRIC B (TAN): 1⅛ yards

FABRIC C (RED): 1½ yards

BACKING: 7⅝ yards

BINDING: ⅞ yard

CUTTING

FABRIC A (AQUA)

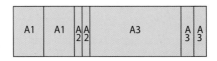

1. Cut 2 strips 25½″ × WOF (selvage to selvage) and sew together end to end; trim A1.

2. Cut 2 strips 6½″ × WOF and sew together end to end; trim A2.

3. Cut 1 piece 40½″ × 74½″.

4. Cut 2 strips 10½″ × WOF and sew together end to end; trim to 74½″.

5. Sew the pieces from Steps 3 and 4 together along the long side to make A3.

A1: 25½″ × 74½″
After some piecing, this will be cut down to A1, A1.1, and A1.2.

A2: 6½″ × 74½″
After some piecing, this will be cut down to A2, A2.1, and A2.2.

A3: 50½″ × 74½″
Cut into *A3:* 50½″ × 45½″;
A3.1: 50½″ × 12½″; and *A3.2:* 50½″ × 16½″.

FABRIC B (TAN)

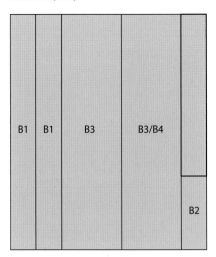

1. Cut 2 strips 4½″ × WOF and sew together end to end; trim B1.

2. Cut 2 strips 10½″ × WOF and sew together end to end; cut B3 and B4.

3. Cut B2.

B1: 4½″ × 74½″
After some piecing, this will be cut down to B1, B1.1, and B1.2.

B2: 4½″ × 12½″

B3: 10½″ × 45½″

B4: 10½″ × 33½″

FABRIC C (RED)

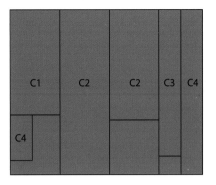

1. Cut 3 strips 12½″ × WOF.

2. Trim a strip from Step 1 to C1. Set aside the leftover strip.

3. Sew together the 2 other 12½″ strips end to end; cut C2.

4. Cut 2 strips 5½″ × WOF.

5. Trim a strip from Step 4 to C3.

6. Trim the scrap from Step 2 to 5½″ × 11″ and sew this scrap to the remaining 5½″-wide strip; cut C4.

C1: 12½″ × 25½″

C2: 12½″ × 66½″

C3: 5½″ × 35½″

C4: 5½″ × 50½″

Photo by Bethany Nauert

Assembling the Quilt Top

Press after each step.

Strips are sewn together, and then those units are cut into sections to make the quilt top.

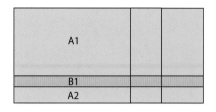

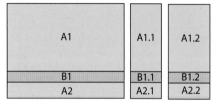

1. Sew A1, B1, and A2.

2. Cut the strip set from Step 1 into 3 units: 45½″ wide, 12½″ wide, and 16½″ wide.

3. Add B3 and A3 to the 45½″-wide unit (Panel 1).

4. Sew C1, B2, and C2 (Panel 2).

5. Sew A1.1 / B1.1 / A2.1 to C3, and then add A1.2 / B1.2 / A2.2 (Panel 3).

6. Sew A3.1 and A3.2 to C4 (Panel 4).

7. Sew Panels 3 and 4 to B4.

8. Sew Panels 1 and 2 together.

9. Sew the 2 halves together to complete the quilt top.

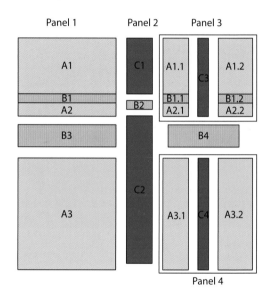

Making the Quilt Back

To make a 100″ × 105″ quilt back, cut 2 pieces 100″ × WOF and remove the selvages. Sew the 2 pieces together along the 100″ edges. Then add 21″ more to the bottom as follows: Cut 3 strips 21½″ × WOF, piece them together, trim to 100″, and sew the long strip to the bottom of the quilt back.

Small Plates

BY ELIZABETH HARTMAN

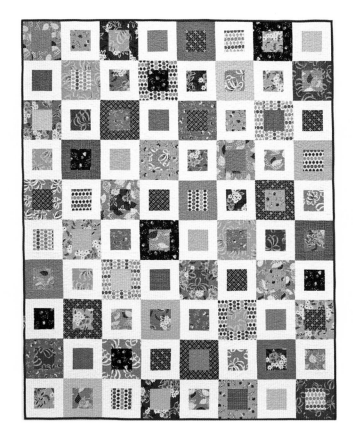

FINISHED BLOCK: 8½″ × 8½″

FINISHED QUILT: 68″ × 85″

One of the most tried and true of contemporary patchwork motifs, the Square-in-Square block creates a fabric "frame" around a center square. Not only does it do a great job of showing off your favorite fabrics, but it's also easy to piece, making it a fantastic choice for beginners.

Made and machine quilted by Elizabeth Hartman

MATERIALS

Yardages are based on fabric that is at least 40″ wide, unless otherwise noted.

DIFFERENT PRINTS (20): ⅜ yard each for quilt blocks and back

NEUTRAL SOLIDS: 2½ yards for quilt blocks and back

BACKING: 5⅓ yards

BINDING: ¾ yard

BATTING: 72″ × 89″

CUTTING

PRINT FABRICS

From *each* of the 20 prints:

Cut 2 strips 2½″ × width of fabric. Subcut each of these strips into 2 pieces 2½″ × 5″, 2 pieces 2½″ × 9″, and 1 piece 2½″ × 10″.

Cut 1 strip 5″ × width of fabric. Subcut *each* strip into 4 squares 5″ × 5″.

You should now have the following print fabrics cut for the quilt construction:

80 squares 5″ × 5″

80 pieces 2½″ × 5″

80 pieces 2½″ × 9″

Cutting continues on page 54

NEUTRAL SOLIDS

Unfold the fabric and trim off the selvage edges.

Cut 2 strips 2½″ × *length* of fabric. Trim each strip to 2½″ × 76½″ long.

Refold the fabric along the width.

Cut 6 strips 5″ × width of fabric. Subcut the strips to make 80 pieces 2½″ × 5″.

Cut 6 strips 9″ × width of fabric. Subcut the strips to make 80 pieces 2½″ × 9″.

You should now have the following cut from the neutral solid fabric for the quilt construction:

80 pieces 2½″ × 5″

80 pieces 2½″ × 9″

BACKING

Cut 5⅓ yards into 2 lengths, each 96″ long, and piece together side by side to make the back.

BINDING

Cut 8 strips 2½″ × width of fabric.

Making the Blocks

All seam allowances are ¼″, and all seams are pressed open unless otherwise noted.

There are 80 blocks in the finished quilt top. Each block is made from a 5″ × 5″ print square and a set of 2 pieces 2½″ × 5″ and 2 pieces 2½″ × 9″.

Half (40) the blocks are made with all print fabrics. We'll call these the print blocks.

The other half (40) are made with a print square and solid pieces. We'll call these the solid blocks.

Print block

Solid block

 tip To ensure that the print fabrics are distributed evenly throughout the quilt, make sure to divide the 5″ squares equally between the print and solid blocks. For instance, if you have four squares cut from each fabric, use two of them to make print blocks and two of them to make solid blocks.

MAKING THE SOLID BLOCKS

1. Use 40 of the 5″ print fabric squares, 80 solid fabric 2½″ × 5″ pieces, and 80 solid fabric 2½″ × 9″ pieces.

2. Sew 2½″ × 5″ pieces of solid fabric to the top and bottom of each square.

3. Sew 2½″ × 9″ pieces of solid fabric to the right and left sides of each block to finish the block.

4. Square up each block to 9″ × 9″.

MAKING THE PRINT BLOCKS

1. Use the 40 remaining 5″ print fabric squares, 80 print fabric 2½″ × 5″ pieces, and 80 print fabric 2½″ × 9″ pieces.

2. Pair each 5″ square with a matching set of 2 pieces 2½″ × 5″ and 2 pieces 2½″ × 9″.

3. Sew the 2½″ × 5″ pieces to the left and right sides of each corresponding square.

4. Sew the 2½″ × 9″ pieces to the top and bottom to finish each block.

5. Square up each block to 9″ × 9″.

tip The strips are sewn onto the print and solid blocks in a different order. This will look better in the finished composition than it would if we made all the seams face the same way.

Print block

Solid block

Making the Quilt Top

1. Lay out the finished blocks in 10 rows of 8 blocks as shown in the quilt top assembly diagram. Alternate the blocks between print and solid to form a checkerboard pattern.

2. Sew each row of 8 blocks together. Sew the rows together to finish the quilt top.

Quilt top assembly

Finishing the Quilt

For details on sandwiching and quilting, refer to Chapter 5: Quilting by Hand and Machine (page 86). For details on binding your project, refer to Binding Your Quilt (page 114).

Chapter 4: Appliqué

Tools and Fabric for Appliqué

BY ALEX ANDERSON

As with any art, craft, or trade, having the right tools and materials makes all the difference in the world. The following pages list and describe what you'll need for a successful appliqué experience.

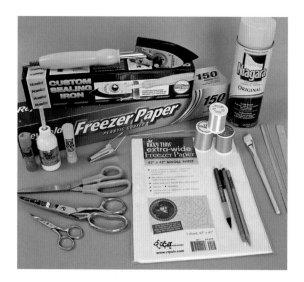

Thread for Hand Appliqué

Many threads work well for hand appliqué. The most common is the 50-weight, 100% cotton thread you use in your sewing machine. It comes in a variety of colors, and you probably already have a good selection in your sewing box. However, there are *many* other threads you may want to try. The Rolls-Royce choice is silk, which buries itself so well in the fabric that you need only a few basic colors, such as light taupe, dark gray, and several primary hues. However, silk thread can be expensive; a wonderful alternative is a high-end

60-weight polyester. Embroidery floss and perle cotton are good choices for hand buttonhole-stitch (blanket-stitch) appliqué.

NOTE *When referring to appliqué shapes, I use the terms "seam allowance" and "turn-under allowance" interchangeably.*

For most hand appliqué, your thread should match (or blend invisibly into) the color of your appliqué shape, not the background. The exceptions are reverse appliqué (page 71), for which the thread should match the overlying fabric, and the hand buttonhole stitch (page 70), which is intended to be visible and for which you might choose thread in a contrasting color as an accent.

Thread for Machine Appliqué

With machine appliqué, you have two thread choices to make: the thread that passes through the needle of the machine and the thread that is wound on the bobbin. You'll also want to choose the best thread for the technique you plan to use.

Top thread   For the invisible appliqué stitch, use a high-quality invisible thread, such as Mono-Poly, or a fine 50-weight cotton in a color to match the appliqué shape. Use jeans thread for the buttonhole (blanket) stitch. Your choice of color for the buttonhole stitch will depend upon whether you want the stitches to be inconspicuous or to contrast with the fabric and thus act as a design element.

Bobbin thread My favorite bobbin thread for the invisible appliqué stitch (including free-motion) is a fine cotton, such as MasterPiece, or a high-end polyester, such as The Bottom Line. For this technique, the bobbin thread should match the color of the background fabric. For the buttonhole stitch, I prefer 50-weight cotton thread to match the top thread.

Needles for Hand Appliqué

Various types of needles are available for hand appliqué, each with its own benefits. For the basic appliqué stitch (page 67), I recommend that you start with size 11 sharps, which are long, slender, easy to maneuver, and easy to find. Other options include straw or milliner's needles, which are slightly longer than sharps. If you are adept at hand quilting and are comfortable with a small needle, you might want to try a betweens quilting needle for your appliqué. For the hand buttonhole (blanket) stitch, choose a needle with a sharp point and an eye large enough to accommodate one strand of perle cotton or two strands of embroidery floss, such as a size 6–8 embroidery or sharps needle.

An important consideration when you choose a needle is the size of the eye. Is it large enough to thread without difficulty? Eye size can vary from brand to brand, so experiment to find not only which type but which brand of needle suits you best.

Needles for Machine Appliqué

The topstitch needle is my hands-down favorite for all machine work—period. It suits a variety of threads, and I don't need to think about what I have in my machine when I sit down to sew. Its large eye is particularly kind to fragile (for example, metallic) and decorative threads. A jeans needle would be my second choice.

Specialty Feet for Machine Appliqué

If machine appliqué is your thing, you'll want to keep a few specialty sewing machine feet close by. For the invisible appliqué stitch (page 72), use an open-toe foot; it allows you to see where you are about to stitch and has a cut out "V" shape on the bottom that gives the stitch somewhere to go. The darning foot is the attachment of choice for free-motion appliqué (page 74).

This foot allows you to steer the fabric, giving you—not the machine—control of the direction.

Darning foot and open-toe foot

Pins

Don't skimp on pins! Look for pins that are short, sharp, and fine. Some quilters like the tiny sequin pins available at craft stores. My favorites are the extra-fine (1⅜″) glass-head pins I use for machine piecing. They are a bit more expensive than other pins, but—believe me—they are worth the investment. Avoid large, bargain-brand quilting pins; they'll get in your way, catching your thread as you sew and potentially leaving holes in your appliqués.

Scissors

Keep three pairs of scissors on hand: one for cutting fabric; one for cutting paper and fusible web; and a small, sharp pair for snipping threads and other cutting.

Marking Tools

There are many options out there for marking on fabric, but my personal favorites are General's White Charcoal pencils, silver Verithin (any style) pencils, and extra-hard lead mechanical pencils. These simple tools allow me to mark a fine line that shows up on most fabrics, and the markings are fairly easy to remove. Whatever marking tool you select, test it first on fabrics you intend to use to be sure you can remove the markings.

Heat-Resistant Template Material

For shapes that must be traced multiple times, it's a good idea to make a template from sturdy material. Although cardboard or card stock will work, a much better choice is the translucent template plastic available at your local quilt shop. Choose a heavy, heat-resistant variety, particularly if you intend to use it for making circles.

Freezer Paper

The two sides of freezer paper—one with a dull, paper finish you can write on, the other coated with plastic that sticks to your fabric when pressed with a hot, dry iron—make it perfect to use for appliqué templates. You can purchase freezer paper by the roll at your local grocery store. Large (42″ × 42″) and small (8½″ × 11″) sheets are available from C&T Publishing.

Lightbox

Unlike many appliquérs, I do not mark the locations of the appliqué shapes on my background fabric. If a pattern is too complicated to arrange by using folded guidelines in the background fabric or by eyeballing it, I place the pattern on a lightbox and use the pattern to position the shapes, securing them to the background fabric with temporary, water-soluble fabric glue.

If you do not have a lightbox, you can substitute a sunny window, or you can place a lamp or flashlight beneath a glass-top table.

Iron and Pressing Surface

Along with the full-size, all-purpose iron you typically use for your quilting projects, you'll find a mini (wand) iron—such as the Hobbico Craft Iron—extremely useful, especially for preparing appliqué shapes with the spray-starch technique (page 61). A mini iron makes maneuvering those turn-under seam allowances *so much* easier!

tip Some quilters reserve a separate iron just for use with their appliqué projects, particularly when these projects involve fusible web or spray starch.

For preparing your appliqué shapes, you'll want a really firm ironing surface so you can get a nice crisp fold on those turned edges. For pressing the finished appliquéd block, use a soft, giving surface, such as a fluffy towel folded double. Press from the reverse side of the block so you don't "smoosh" the appliqué shapes flat. (For pressing pieced blocks, I recommend a hard surface.)

Temporary Fabric Glue

Look for a water-soluble temporary fabric glue to secure your prepared appliqué shapes to the background fabric until you are ready to appliqué them in place. I use this glue for both machine and hand projects.

Spray Starch and Brush

You'll need spray starch and a brush if you choose the spray-starch method (page 61) to prepare your appliqué shapes. You can use any generic spray starch found on the grocery store shelf, in either regular or extra strength. Be sure you use starch and not spray sizing, which doesn't seem to do the job as well. For the brush, you can use either a small paintbrush or a small foam makeup brush.

Glue stick

Obviously, a glue stick is a must-have for the glue stick-basting method (page 62) of preparing your appliqué shapes. The brand is unimportant as long as the glue is water-soluble.

Stiletto

A stiletto is a simple, sharply pointed tool that is essential for coaxing the seam allowance over the template when you are working with a mini iron to prepare appliqué shapes with the spray-starch method (page 61). Trust me: Your fingers will thank you!

Lightweight Fusible Web

Fusible web is a heat-activated, synthetic fiber that, when placed between two layers of fabric and pressed, bonds the layers together. You can purchase fusible web in packaged sheets or off the bolt. Many brands are available; my personal favorite is Lite Steam-A-Seam 2. It is lightweight, it adheres but can be repositioned until pressed for a permanent bond, and it is easy to stitch through. Whichever brand of fusible web you select, make sure to read the manufacturer's directions for use (usually printed on the wrapper), particularly with regard to pressing.

Stabilizer

Stabilizer, which is similar to interfacing, helps keep your machine buttonhole (blanket) stitches from puckering the fabric. Choose a tear-away version that you can remove easily after the appliqué shapes are stitched.

Bias-Tape Maker

When used with your iron, a bias-tape maker is a handy notion that enables you to make folded bias strips from any fabric you like. The tool comes in various sizes, so you can make ready-to-stitch vines and stems in the width you need for your project.

Bias Presser Bars

Bias presser bars are narrow bars, made from either metal or vinyl, that come in various widths—typically ⅛″ to 1¾″. Although the product name usually includes the word "bias," you can use them for stems cut from the straight grain as well.

Fray Check

Fray Check is clear liquid that helps stop fraying on the raw edges of appliqué shapes. It is especially helpful when you are appliquéing very sharp inside ("V") angles, as for hearts and deep scallops, until you become confident with the security of your stitches. (Using a toothpick to apply the Fray Check will help you control the amount of the liquid.) As with marking tools, be sure to test it on the fabrics you intend to use.

Fabric

As with any other quilting project, you'll want to put the very best fabrics into your appliqué quilts. If you are new to appliqué, I suggest that you start with *high-quality* 100% cotton fabrics—the kind you'll find at your local quilt shop. I can't stress the words "high-quality" enough. Trust me on this: you don't want to struggle with fabric that frays excessively or puckers or runs when the finished quilt is laundered.

Preparing for Appliqué

BY ALEX ANDERSON

Appliqué takes a bit of preparation, both for the individual appliqué shapes and for the appliqué background. This preparation isn't difficult; read through the following pages to determine which methods will work best for you and your particular project.

PREPARING THE INDIVIDUAL APPLIQUÉS

There are several ways to prepare the individual appliqué shapes. Some methods work for one specific appliqué technique, and others work for multiple techniques. Some methods are appropriate for handwork only, some for machine appliqué only, and others for both. To help you quickly identify an appropriate technique, I've accompanied each section with the appropriate icon of a needle and thread, a sewing machine, or both.

Preparing for Needle-Turn Appliqué

1. To make a set of templates, trace each pattern given with the project onto sturdy template material. Cut out the templates on the traced lines.

Trace around template.

2. Place each template on the right side of the desired appliqué fabric. Trace around the template with your preferred marking tool.

3. Cut out the appliqué shape, adding a little less than ¼″ (a "scant" ¼″, approximately ³⁄₁₆″) turn-under allowance.

Cut out shape.

Preparing for Paper-Basted Appliqué

You will need to reverse the pattern for paper-basting methods. When a shape will overlap with another shape, you do not need to prepare the raw edge that will be hidden.

THREAD BASTING

For the thread-basting method, the freezer-paper template remains in place while you stitch the appliqué shape to the background and is then removed after the stitching is complete (see the note in Basic Stitch for Needle-Turn or Paper-Basted Appliqué, page 67).

1. Reverse the patterns given with the project, and trace them onto the dull (paper) side of freezer paper. You will need a freezer-paper template for each individual appliqué shape. Cut out the freezer-paper templates on the traced lines.

2. Place each freezer-paper template shiny side down on the wrong side of the desired appliqué fabric. Be sure to leave at least ½″ between shapes to allow for the turn-under allowance. Press to adhere the templates to the fabric.

Place freezer-paper templates onto fabric and press.

3. Cut out the appliqué shapes, adding a scant ¼˝ (approximately ³⁄₁₆˝) for the turn-under allowance.

Cut out.

4. Roll the edges of the fabric over the freezer-paper template, and baste with a needle and thread.

Roll edge of fabric over freezer paper and baste.

Wrong side

Right side

NOTE *For shapes with deep inside curves, use very sharp scissors to clip just to edge of the freezer paper. (Consider applying a drop of Fray Check to the fabric with a toothpick.)*

Clip inside curve.

BASTING WITH SPRAY STARCH

I love the spray-starch basting method; it has become my favorite way to prepare shapes for both hand and machine appliqué. Not only is it easy, but the freezer paper is removed before the shape is stitched to the background, so you can reuse the freezer-paper templates many times. Although you'll want to use one of the techniques described in Preparing Circles (page 63) to prepare your smallest round shapes, the spray-starch method works well for larger circles.

NOTE *You must be willing to immerse the finished project in water to remove the spray starch because starch left in the fabric may attract silverfish.*

1. Layer 2 pieces of freezer paper, shiny sides down, and press them so that the layers adhere to each other. The double thickness gives more rigidity and makes turning over the edges easier. Reverse each pattern piece given with the project, and trace it onto the dull (paper) side of the layered freezer paper. Cut out the freezer-paper templates on the traced lines.

2. Press the layered templates, shiny side down, to the wrong side of the desired appliqué fabric. Cut out the appliqué shapes, adding a scant ¼˝

(approximately ³⁄₁₆″) turn-under allowance.

Press template onto fabric and cut out.

3. Spray a bit of starch into the cap of the starch can. (You can water the starch down a bit if you like.) Using a small paintbrush (or a foam makeup brush) and working with the paper side up, apply the starch to the exposed turn-under allowance. Be sure to use enough starch to saturate the fabric. (It's okay if you get some starch on the paper.)

Brush starch onto turn-under allowance.

4. Using a stiletto in one hand and a small wand iron in the other hand, coax the turn-under allowance over the edge of the freezer-paper template. When

you are finished, turn the prepared shape over to check your results. Make any minor adjustments in the edges now; once the shape is thoroughly pressed in Step 6 (below), you will not be able to make any adjustments.

Fold turn-under allowance over template.

5. When you have finished turning the edges, press the prepared appliqué thoroughly on both sides.

6. Lift a small edge of the turn-under allowance, and remove the freezer paper. Re-press the appliqué to ensure that the starch is completely dry. Your appliqué is now ready to stitch, and you can reuse the template multiple times!

Remove template.

GLUE STICK-BASTING

Glue stick-basting is another simple method for paper-basting appliqué shapes over freezer-paper templates. With this method, however, you will need to make one template for each individual appliqué shape. The template remains in place while you stitch the shape to the background and is then removed after the stitching is complete (see the note in Basic Stitch for Needle-Turn or Paper-Basted Appliqué, page 67).

1. Prepare the appliqué shapes as described in Thread Basting, Steps 1–3 (page 60).

2. Using a water-soluble glue stick, apply glue to the turn-under allowance and roll the fabric over the paper template, using your fingers to maneuver the fabric smoothly over the edges of the template.

Apply glue and roll fabric over template.

Smooth fabric along edges with your fingers.

3. After you have appliquéd the shapes using your preferred hand or machine method, cut away the background, spritz the fabric with cool water to release the glue, and remove the template (see the note in Basic Stitch for Needle-Turn or Paper-Basted Appliqué, page 67).

Preparing Circles

My favorite method for preparing circles for appliqué is the "shower cap" method.

1. Trace the circle pattern given with the project onto heat-resistant template material. Cut out the template on the traced lines. Go for perfection here; if the plastic circle is wonky, your finished fabric circle will be, too.

tip Precut circle templates are available in a variety of sizes. You might want to check your local quilt shop or an online source for the sizes you need. Another option is to visit your local craft or scrapbooking store and purchase a circle cutter—it makes quick work of cutting your own templates from heat-resistant plastic.

2. Place the circle template on the wrong side of the desired appliqué fabric. Use your preferred marking tool to trace around the template.

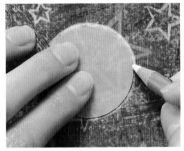

Trace circle onto fabric.

3. Remove the template and cut out the appliqué shape, adding a scant ¼″ (approximately ³⁄₁₆″) turn-under allowance.

Cut out.

4. Knot one end of a single strand of sturdy thread. Beginning with a backstitch, sew around the perimeter of

the fabric circle with a running stitch, making sure to keep the stitching within the area between the traced line and the raw edge of the fabric circle.

Sew.

5. Replace the template, and pull the thread to gather the fabric turn-under allowance around the template. Smooth out any folds, saturate the shape on both sides with spray starch, and use a *very hot* steam iron to press the fabric circle. Allow the starch to dry *completely*.

Pull thread to gather.

6. Loosen the gathering thread, and carefully remove the template. Once again, gently pull the gathering thread so the fabric forms a perfect circle.

Loosen thread and remove template.

Preparing for Raw-Edge Appliqué

The raw-edge appliqué method is used to prepare appliqué shapes for hand or machine buttonhole (blanket) stitch. With this method, you do not add a seam allowance to the appliqué shapes. The shapes are prepared using a lightweight fusible web and are bonded to the back-ground with an iron. As you did for the paper-basting preparation method, you will need to reverse the pattern for the raw-edge appliqué method.

OPTION 1: USING A TEMPLATE

1. To make a set of templates, reverse each pattern given with the project, and trace it onto sturdy template material. Cut out the templates on the traced lines.

2. Follow the manufacturer's directions to bond the fusible web to the wrong side of the desired appliqué fabric.

3. Place the template on the paper side of the fusible web that you fused to the fabric in Step 2, and trace around the template with a sharp pencil.

Trace shape.

4. Cut out the appliqué shape on the traced line.

Cut out.

OPTION 2: TRACING THE SHAPE

1. Reverse each pattern given with the project, and trace it onto the paper side of fusible web.

2. Cut out each shape approximately ¼˝ from the drawn line.

Trace shape onto fusible web and cut out.

3. Follow the manufacturer's directions to bond the fusible web to the wrong side of the desired appliqué fabric.

Fuse to fabric.

4. Cut out the appliqué shape on the traced line.

Cut out.

Preparing Vines and Stems

For curving stems and vines, cut strips on the bias (diagonal) of the fabric. Bias strips stretch nicely to create curves. For straight stems, which don't need to bend, you can cut the necessary strips from the straight (lengthwise or crosswise) grain of the fabric.

1. Use your ruler and rotary cutter to straighten the edge of the desired appliqué fabric. Place the fabric on your cutting mat, aligning the straightened edge of the fabric with a line on the mat. Position your ruler so that the 45° marking is aligned with the straight edge of the fabric. Make a cut.

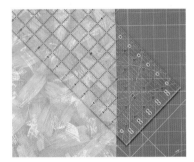

Position ruler and cut.

2. Move the ruler over to the cut width given in the project instructions. Line up the long edge of the ruler with the trimmed 45° fabric edge.

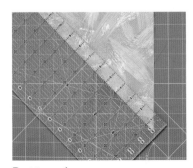

Position ruler.

3. Cut the strip. Continue cutting strips until you have the number (or total length) of strips required for your project.

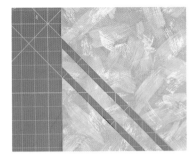

Cut.

USING THE SEW-AND-FLIP METHOD

Formula Cut a bias strip twice the desired width of the finished strip plus ½˝.

1. Cut bias strips to the width and length listed in the project cutting instructions. With wrong sides together, fold the strip in half lengthwise, and press.

2. Hand or machine stitch the strip to the background fabric ¼˝ from the raw edges of the strip.

Fold strip in half, press, and stitch.

3. Carefully press the folded edge of the strip over the seam, so the strip covers the raw edges.

If the strip is not wide enough to cover the raw edges, trim the seam allowance.

Press. Trim if necessary.

4. Use your preferred appliqué stitch to stitch the folded edge in place.

Stitch.

USING A BIAS-TAPE MAKER

Formula Cut a bias strip twice the desired width of the finished strip.

Bias-tape makers come in a variety of sizes. Choose one that will give you the finished size you desire. My advice is to follow the instructions on the packaging of the bias-tape maker; however, here are a few tips to help you along.

• Cut the leading end of the strip at an angle so it is easier to feed into the tool.

• Spray the strip *lightly* with spray starch, and crumple the strip gently in your hands to distribute the starch evenly.

- Use a stiletto to maneuver the strip.

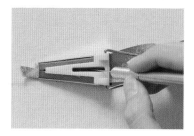

- Secure the angled end of the strip to the ironing board with a straight pin. With one hand holding the iron over the folded end, gently pull the tool across the fabric strip with your other hand, pressing the strip into shape.

- After you've used the tool, use straight pins to coax the pre-pared strips into gentle curves on your ironing surface.

USING BIAS PRESSER BARS

Formula Cut a bias strip at least twice the width of the bias presser bar plus a scant ⅝˝ for metal bars and a generous ⅝˝ for vinyl bars.

1. Cut bias strips to the width and length listed in the project cutting instructions. If necessary, piece the strips with diagonal seams to achieve the required length.

2. With wrong sides together, fold the strip in half length-wise, and press. Carefully stitch ¼˝ from the long raw edge as shown to the left.

3. Insert the desired bias presser bar into the fabric tube, and roll the seam to the underside of the bar, trimming the seam allow-ance if necessary. Press the strip. (I like to use steam.) After each section is pressed, move the bar down the fabric tube, and press again. Take care if you are using a metal bias presser bar because it will get very hot.

Roll seam to underside and press.

PREPARING THE BACKGROUND FOR APPLIQUÉ

I recommend that you cut your background blocks slightly oversize (1˝ or 2˝ larger in both length and width) to accommodate the slight shrinkage, or drawing up, that can occur as you appliqué the shapes.

1. Mark the center point of the background block and the vertical and horizontal (and sometimes the diagonal) axis points. These guidelines are extremely helpful in positioning the appliqués on the background area. You can mark the back-ground block by folding it in half vertically and then creasing it with your fingers, or by using a pressing tool or an iron (lightly). Unfold the block, and repeat to fold and crease the block hori-zontally and, if desired, along both diagonals. You can also use the vertical/horizontal folding method to "mark" border strips for appliqué.

tip I do not mark the design on the background. Instead, I either eyeball the placement of the appliqués or use a lightbox to position and glue the appliqué shapes in place using temporary water-soluble fabric glue.

2. Layer the appliqué shapes from the bottom up, that is, in the order you will be stitch-ing them. To help you, I've labeled the pieces for the project appliqués in alphabetical order, so you can place piece A first, then piece B, and so on. Place a few dots of the temporary fabric glue around the edges on the wrong side of each shape (and a few in the center, if you like), and gently finger-press the shape to the background.

Place temporary fabric glue.

3. Layer the shapes as appropriate.

Layer shapes.

tip When you are placing the shapes on the appliqué border for a square quilt, arrange the motifs on one border, and then layer the remaining borders one by one to duplicate the arrangement.

4. Once you've finished with the appliqué, trim the block to the finished size *plus ¼˝ seam allowance* all around, making sure to keep the appliqué design centered in the block. The cutting instructions for the various projects allow for this seam allowance.

Hand Appliqué Techniques

BY ALEX ANDERSON

If you love the meditative quality of handwork, this is the section for you! Read through the options, choose an appropriate preparation method (page 60), and enjoy the process. A small lap desk, like the type you might find in a book or stationery store, makes a great surface for hand appliqué. Make sure you have ample light, and stop occasionally to rest your eyes and stretch and flex your fingers.

BASIC STITCH FOR NEEDLE-TURN OR PAPER-BASTED APPLIQUÉ

MATERIALS

50-WEIGHT THREAD: 100% cotton, silk, or high-end polyester to match or blend with appliqué shapes

SIZE 11 NEEDLE: sharps, straw or milliner's, or betweens quilting

SMALL, SHARP-POINTED SCISSORS

THIMBLE (*optional*)

FRAY CHECK

Typically, if you are right-handed, you will stitch right to left, or counterclockwise. Lefties usually stitch in the reverse direction: left to right, or clockwise. The photos show you both ways.

The following instructions for the basic appliqué stitch are the same for needle-turn or paper-basted appliqué. The difference is that with needle-turn appliqué, you turn under the seam allowances as you stitch the shapes to the background, whereas with paper-basted appliqué, the raw edges are turned under before you stitch the shape to the background. The instructional photos show the needle-turn method.

NOTE *If you have used the thread-basting (page 60) or glue stick–basting preparation method (page 62), you will need to remove the freezer-paper templates after the shapes have been stitched to the background. To do so, remove the basting threads, or moisten the shape to loosen the glue from the glue stick. Use small, sharp-pointed scissors to make a slit in the background fabric behind the appliqué shape as described in Cutting Away the Background (page 71). Remove the freezer-paper template. If you wish, cut away the background fabric inside the shape, leaving a scant ¼˝ (approximately ³⁄₁₆˝) seam allowance.*

1. Thread your needle, knotting the end of the thread. The best place to start stitching is on a straight or slightly curved edge. Fold under the edge of the shape, on the marked line, where you will begin stitching. Turn under only the amount of fabric you can control and stitch at one time (about ½˝). From the back of the shape, come through the fabric with the needle exactly at the folded edge you want to stitch. The knot will be hidden on the back of the fabric.

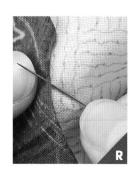

2. Reinsert the needle straight down into the background fabric, right beside the point at which the needle emerged. Travel approximately ⅛˝ under the background fabric, and then come back up again through the background fabric and the folded edge. Ideally, you want to catch the underside of the fold so the stitch is hidden under the fold. To complete the stitch, pull the thread just taut—not too tight, not too loose.

3. Continue using the tip of the needle to turn the edge of the fabric under as you go.

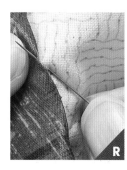

4. When you are finished stitching the appliqué shape, insert the needle straight down into the background fabric, and pull the needle so the thread is taut. Take a minute stitch in the background fabric behind the appliqué shape, as close as possible to the last appliqué stitch.

5. Wrap the thread around the needle twice, and pull the thread through the wraps.

6. Insert the needle through the background fabric between the appliqué and background layers, and come up about ½˝ from the insertion point. Trim off the thread. The tail will be hidden between the layers.

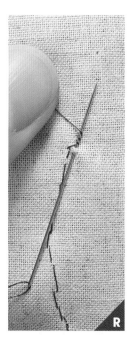

Curves

Use small, sharp-pointed scissors to clip the curved edge of the turn-under allowance, just to the marked line. The tighter the curve, the more clips you will need to make. As you appliqué the curve, make the stitches even closer together than usual.

Points

1. Stitch up to the marked point using the basic appliqué stitch (see Basic Stitch for Needle-Turn or Paper-Basted Appliqué, page 67). When you reach the point, bring the needle up through the background and the appliqué shape right at the tip of the marked point.

2. Take a stitch exactly at the point

3. If necessary, carefully trim away a bit of the excess seam allowance underneath the area of the appliqué shape that you just stitched. The sharper the point, the smaller you will want the seam allowance to be.

Trim excess seam allowance, if necessary.

4. Use the tip of your needle to gently turn under the seam allowance on the other side of the point. (Turning the seam allowance under completely at the point will require two or more turns.) Take an extra stitch to anchor the point, pulling the thread taut (not tight) to help define the point. Continue stitching away from the point with the basic appliqué stitch.

Inside ("V") Angles

1. Starting on a straight or slightly curved edge, use the basic appliqué stitch (see Basic Stitch for Needle-Turn or Paper-Basted Appliqué, page 67) to begin sewing the appliqué shape to the background. Stop stitching just before you reach the "V," and use very sharp scissors to clip all the way to the marked turn-under line, directly toward the "V."

2. Take 1 or 2 tiny anchoring stitches right at the "V" to keep the clipped turn-under allowance from fraying.

3. Resume stitching on the other side of the "V" with the basic appliqué stitch.

BUTTONHOLE-STITCH (BLANKET-STITCH) APPLIQUÉ

MATERIALS

EMBROIDERY FLOSS OR PERLE COTTON THREAD in a color that contrasts with or matches the appliqué shape, depending upon the effect you desire

NEEDLE WITH A LARGE EYE AND SHARP POINT (such as size 6–8 embroidery or sharps)

SMALL, SHARP-POINTED SCISSORS

THIMBLE (*optional*)

With buttonhole-stitch appliqué, there are no seam allowances to turn under, and the end result is less formal looking than that achieved with the needle-turn and paper-basting methods. You can choose threads to match the appliqués for a subtle effect, or have fun introducing threads in contrasting colors to add an extra layer of design.

1. Thread your needle with 1 strand of perle cotton or 2 strands of embroidery floss. Knot the thread.

2. From the wrong side of the background fabric, bring the threaded needle up through the background fabric at the raw edge of the appliqué shape. (The knot will be hidden behind the fabric.) Hold the thread against the fabric and away from the shape with your thumb. Insert the needle into the appliqué shape approximately ¼" from where the needle came out. Reemerge from the background fabric at the raw edge of the appliqué, bringing the tip of the needle over the working thread. Pull the thread taut (not tight) to bring the stitch into place. Continue stitching in this manner all the way around the shape.

3. Knot off as in Basic Stitch for Needle-Turn or Paper-Basted Appliqué, Step 5 (page 68).

Points and Inside "V" Angles

When you reach a point or corner, make a small anchor stitch before proceeding to the adjacent side.

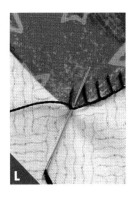

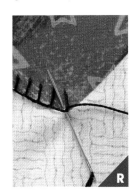

CUTTING AWAY THE BACKGROUND

Once a shape has been appliquéd to the background, you'll need to decide whether to cut away the background fabric from behind the shape. If the shape is small, dark, and only one layer deep, such as a small leaf, I tend not to bother. However, if the shape is multilayered or if an underlayer might shadow through, cutting away the background is a sensible step. Use small, sharp-pointed scissors to carefully make a slit in the background fabric behind the appliquéd shape. Cut away the background fabric inside the

Cut away background.

shape, leaving a scant ¼″ (approximately ³⁄₁₆″) seam allowance.

REVERSE APPLIQUÉ

When your appliqué design includes rounded shapes or shapes that should appear to recede, reverse appliqué may be the answer. As its name implies, this easy technique is just the reverse of traditional appliqué. Rather than stitching the appliqué shape on top of another fabric, you layer the fabrics in such a way that when you cut away the top fabric in the desired shape, you reveal the appliqué fabric underneath.

1. Trace onto sturdy template material the pattern for the shape that you plan to reverse appliqué. Cut out the template on the traced lines.

2. Place the template on the right side of the *top* fabric, and trace around the shape with your preferred (non-permanent) marking tool.

Trace onto fabric.

3. Cut out the shape *inside* the traced line, leaving a scant ¼˝ (approximately ³⁄₁₆˝) turn-under allowance. Layer the top fabric over the right side of the fabric you want to reveal, and pin or baste.

Cut out.

4. Select thread to match the *top* fabric, and use the needle-turn method (page 67) to turn under and stitch the top fabric to the underlying layer.

Stitch.

Machine Appliqué Techniques

BY ALEX ANDERSON

When it comes to options for machine appliqué, "we've come a long way, baby!" With the innovations in sewing machine technology and with the wide variety of threads and notions available, machine appliqué is easier and more rewarding than ever.

INVISIBLE APPLIQUÉ STITCH

With just a little practice, you can give your machine work the look of beautiful hand-stitched appliqué.

Machines made by different manufacturers have different stitches to accomplish the invisible appliqué stitch. For example, on your machine, the stitch may be called the blind hemstitch, the overlock stitch, the hand-look appliqué stitch, or something similar.

Refer to your machine's manual, and become familiar with what your machine can do. Don't be afraid to experiment. The key is to find a stitch that will take a few (two to three) small straight stitches along the outer edge of the appliqué shape and then take a bite into and out of the shape before continuing. You may want to shorten the stitch length and narrow the stitch width a bit; you want the bite to be as small as possible and still secure the appliqué shape.

I like to set my needle to the far right position and use the inside edge of the presser foot as a guide. Depending upon your machine, doing so may require that you mirror image the stitch.

MATERIALS

TOP THREAD: high-quality invisible or fine cotton in a color to match the appliqué shape *(In the following photographs, contrasting thread was used so stitches would be visible.)*

BOBBIN THREAD: fine cotton or high-end polyester to match the background fabric

NEEDLE: topstitch or jeans

OPEN-TOE FOOT

SMALL, SHARP-POINTED SCISSORS

1. Attach the open-toe foot to your machine. Choose the appropriate stitch on your machine, and make any necessary adjustments.

2. Starting on a straight or slightly curved edge, position the needle right over the spot where you plan to start stitching. Lower the presser foot. Holding onto the top thread, take one complete stitch, so the needle returns to its highest position. In the following photographs, contrasting thread was used so stitches would be visible. Your thread should match your appliqué shape.

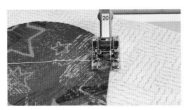

Take one complete stitch.

3. Without raising the presser foot, gently tug the top thread to pull a loop of bobbin thread to the fabric surface. Pull the tail of the bobbin thread through to the surface.

Pull top thread to bring bobbin thread to surface.

 tip If your bobbin hook has an eye, thread the bobbin thread through it. Doing so helps pull down the top thread, enhancing the look of the finished stitch.

4. Engage the needle-down feature, if your machine has one. Insert the needle into the background fabric right beside the shape, and begin stitching. The machine will take a few small straight stitches and will then take a V-shaped bite into the appliqué shape.

Stitch.

5. To end, pull the thread tails through to the back, and tie them off. *Or* reduce the stitch length and width to 0, take a few stitches in place, and carefully trim the thread tails. Your stitches may be visible at this stage, but they will become virtually invisible once the quilt is machine quilted.

Points

For a point (or an outside corner), stitch right to the tip of the point, making sure to stop with the needle down on the *inside* edge of the appliqué, having taken the first half of the V-shaped bite. Lift the presser foot, pivot, lower the foot, and resume stitching on the other side of the point.

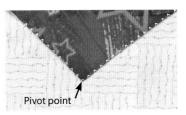

Pivot point

Points

Inside "V" Angles

For an inside "V" angle, stitch right to the angle, this time making sure to stop with the needle down *outside* the edge of the appliqué shape, immediately after having taken the second half of the V-shaped bite. Lift the presser foot, pivot, lower the foot, and resume stitching on the other side of the angle.

Inside "V" angle

FREE-MOTION APPLIQUÉ

MATERIALS

TOP THREAD: high-quality invisible or fine cotton in a color to match the appliqué shape

BOBBIN THREAD: fine cotton or high-end polyester to match the background fabric

NEEDLE: topstitch or jeans

DARNING FOOT

SMALL, SHARP-POINTED SCISSORS

Some years ago, I had the privilege of taking a private machine-quilting lesson with Margaret Gair, a marvelous local quilting instructor. As a bonus, she shared this terrific machine appliqué technique. It is a bit more time consuming than the invisible appliqué stitch method (page 72) but gives you more control. Rather than having the machine create the stitch, *you* manipulate the fabric to do what

the invisible appliqué stitch does. Rather than creating a V-shaped stitch, you stitch in and out of the appliqué fabric with a tiny, straight-line bite. The smaller the bite, the finer the results.

You can do this free-motion work with the feed dogs engaged or dropped. Personally, I prefer not to drop the feed dogs for this technique. I feel that leaving the feed dogs engaged gives me more control.

1. Attach the darning foot to your machine. If you wish, drop the feed dogs. Pull up the bobbin thread and engage the needle-down feature, if your machine has one.

tip If your machine has two spool pins (horizontal or vertical), and if the top thread is stacked on the spool, use the vertical spool pin. If the thread is cross-wound (crisscrossed), use the horizontal spool pin.

Cross-wound spool (*left*), stacked spool (*right*)

2. Starting on a straight or slightly curved edge, insert the needle into the background fabric right beside the raw edge. Take 2 or 3 straight stitches, and then take a tiny bite straight into and then out of the appliqué shape. Continue stitching.

3. Finish off as described in Invisible Appliqué Stitch, Step 5 (page 73).

RAW-EDGE APPLIQUÉ WITH BUTTONHOLE (BLANKET) STITCH

MATERIALS

TOP THREAD: jeans thread in a color that contrasts with or matches the appliqué fabric, depending upon the effect you desire

BOBBIN THREAD: 50-weight cotton to match the top thread

NEEDLE: topstitch or jeans

OPEN-TOE FOOT

TEAR-AWAY STABILIZER

SMALL, SHARP-POINTED SCISSORS

The raw-edge appliqué with buttonhole (blanket) stitch technique for the machine has all the benefits of its hand counterpart. Experiment to find the stitch width and length that give you the desired result, keeping in mind the size of the appliqué shapes. If you prefer, you can substitute a satin stitch or one of the other decorative stitches on your machine for the buttonhole (blanket) stitch. Just make sure you choose a foot suited for the stitch.

1. Back the area behind the appliqué with a tear-away stabilizer to keep the stitches from puckering.

2. Attach the open-toe foot to your machine. Move the machine needle to the far right position, and select the buttonhole stitch on your machine.

Set the stitch length and width as desired, and if necessary, reverse the direction of the stitch. Pull up the bobbin thread, and engage the needle-down feature.

3. Starting on a straight or slightly curved edge, insert the needle into the background fabric, and begin stitching.

Stitch.

4. Finish off as described in Invisible Appliqué Stitch, Step 5 (page 73).

Points

1. For a point (or an outside corner), stop stitching as you approach the point, and use the hand wheel for control as you make the next few stitches. You may need to manipulate both the stitch *and* the background fabric a bit so the needle enters the fabric exactly at the point.

Stop stitching at point.

2. Leaving the needle in the down position, pivot the fabric, and take the bite stitch so that it divides the angle in half.

Pivot and make one stitch at point.

3. Return the needle to the background fabric, pivot, and continue stitching.

Inside "V" Angles

1. For an inside "V" angle, stop stitching when your needle

enters the background fabric at the inside angle. Once again, you may need to manipulate both the stitch and the background fabric so that the needle enters at the correct place.

Stop stitching at inside angle.

2. Leaving the needle in the down position, pivot the fabric, and take the bite stitch so that it divides the inside "V" angle in half.

Pivot and make one stitch at inside angle.

3. Return the needle to the background fabric, pivot, and continue stitching.

Practice Projects: Appliqué

Ranging from traditional to contemporary, these appliqué projects (pages 76–85) will help you practice the techniques you've learned throughout this guide.

Rainbow Petals

BY COREY YODER

FINISHED BLOCK: 8″ × 12″

FINISHED QUILT: 48½″ × 60½″

Pieced by Corey Yoder, quilted by
Jody Hershberger

Fabrics: Simply Color by
Vanessa Christenson, Cuzco by
Kate Spain, and Sew Stitchy by
Aneela Hoey, all for Moda Fabrics

MATERIALS

PETALS: ⅛ yard each of 25 different prints
or 38 precut 10″ × 10″ squares (layer cake)

BACKGROUND AND SASHING: 3 yards

BINDING: ½ yard

BACKING: 3¼ yards

FUSIBLE WEB: 3½ yards (based on 17″ width)

BATTING: 56″ × 68″ piece

CUTTING

BACKGROUND AND SASHING FABRIC:

Cut 9 strips 8½″ × width of fabric;
subcut into 25 rectangles 8½″ × 12½″.

Cut 7 strips 2½″ × width of fabric, trim the selvages,
sew end to end, press the seams open, and cut 4 strips
2½″ × 60½″.

BINDING: Cut 6 strips 2¼″ × width of fabric.

BACKING: Cut 2 pieces 57″ × width of fabric. Sew together
the pieces to form a horizontal seam in the backing.

Construction

PETALS

Refer to Preparing for Appliqué (page 60) as needed.

1. Use the petal pattern (at right) to trace 150 petals onto the fusible web (page 64).

2. Cut out the petals.

3. Fuse the petals to the wrong side of the fabrics: 6 petals per ⅛ yard or 4 petals per 10″ square.

4. Cut out the fabric petals, remove the paper backing, and set them aside.

BLOCKS

Note: All sewing is done right sides together with a ¼″ seam allowance, unless otherwise noted.

Lightly finger-press each rectangle in half lengthwise to mark the center.

ADDING THE APPLIQUÉ

1. For each block, fuse 3 pairs of petals an equal distance apart. Use the creased centerline to help with placement. Allow a ¼″ seam allowance around the perimeter of the block.

2. Finish the appliqué edges as desired. Begin and end the stitching at the X. Stitch the outer edges and then the inner edges of each pair. Make 25 blocks 8½″ × 12½″.

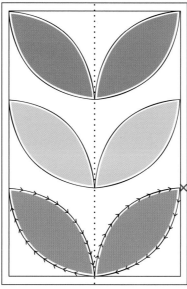

Petal placement and appliqué stitching guide

Rainbow Petals Petal

QUILT TOP ASSEMBLY

1. Sew together the blocks into 5 columns of 5 blocks each. Press the seams in one direction.

2. Join together the columns with the 2½″ × 60½″ sashing strips. Press the seams away from the sashing strips.

FINISHING

For details on sandwiching and quilting, refer to Chapter 5: Quilting by Hand and Machine (page 86). For details on binding your project, refer to Binding Your Quilt (page 114).

Quilt assembly

Hearts and Flowers

BY ALEX ANDERSON

FINISHED BLOCK: 23″ × 12″

FINISHED WALLHANGING: 33″ × 22″

Hearts and Flowers *is a great little project for practicing or perfecting your appliqué technique. Originally created for a cruise in the Baltic Sea, it includes all the basics: bias stems, circles, and inner and outer curves.*

Designed, pieced, and appliquéd by Alex Anderson; machine quilted by Pam Vieira-McGinnis

MATERIALS

Fabric amounts are based on a 42″ fabric width. Fat quarters measure approximately 18″ × 22″.

CREAM TONE-ON-TONE PRINT: ½ yard for appliqué background*

GREEN TONE-ON-TONE PRINT: 1 fat quarter for vine and stem appliqués

ASSORTED GREEN PRINTS: Scraps for leaf (A) appliqués

ASSORTED RED PRINTS: Scraps for large heart (B), tulip (F and F-reverse), and berry (G) appliqués

ASSORTED BLUE PRINTS: Scraps for small heart (C), tulip (D), and flower petal (H) appliqués

ASSORTED GOLDEN YELLOW PRINTS: Scraps for tulip (E) and flower center (I) appliqués

GOLDEN YELLOW TONE-ON-TONE PRINT: ¼ yard for inner border

RED-AND-BLUE PRINT: 1 yard for outer border

BLUE TONE-ON-TONE PRINT: ⅓ yard for binding

BACKING: ⅞ yard of fabric

BATTING: 38″ × 27″ piece

* You can piece the background from 2–4 assorted cream prints.

CUTTING

All measurements include ¼″ seam allowances. Cut all strips on the crosswise grain of the fabric (selvage to selvage) unless otherwise noted. Refer to Preparing the Individual Appliqués (page 60) for guidance as needed.

CREAM TONE-ON-TONE PRINT: Cut 1 rectangle 25″ × 14″.*

GREEN TONE-ON-TONE PRINT: Cut bias strips to make vines and stems with a finished width of ⅜″ (see Preparing Vines and Stems, page 64).

ASSORTED GREEN PRINTS: Cut *a total of* 10 piece A.

ASSORTED RED PRINTS:

Cut *a total of* 1 piece B.

Cut *a total of* 1 each of piece F and piece F reverse.

Cut *a total of* 3 piece G.

ASSORTED BLUE PRINTS

Cut *a total of* 1 piece C.

Cut *a total of* 1 piece D.

Cut *a total of* 8 piece H.

ASSORTED GOLDEN YELLOW PRINTS

Cut *a total of* 1 piece E.

Cut *a total of* 2 piece I.

GOLDEN YELLOW TONE-ON-TONE PRINT

Cut 2 strips 1¼″ × 12½″.

Cut 2 strips 1¼″ × 25″.

RED-AND-BLUE PRINT

Cut 2 strips 4½″ × 14″ from the lengthwise grain.

Cut 2 strips 4½″ × 33″ from the lengthwise grain.

BLUE TONE-ON-TONE PRINT: Cut 4 strips 2⅛″ × the fabric width.

* This rectangle is cut slightly oversize and will be trimmed when the appliqué is complete.

APPLIQUÉING THE BLOCKS

Refer to Preparing for Appliqué (page 60) and to Hand Appliqué Techniques (page 67) or Machine Appliqué Techniques (page 72) for guidance as needed.

Prepare 2 stems 7″ long and 1 stem 2″ long using the green bias strips.

Appliqué Placement

1. Fold the 25″ × 14″ cream rectangle in half horizontally and vertically. Finger-press.

2. Position the bias vines and stem from Appliquéing the Blocks (above), 10 leaf (A) appliqués, 1 large heart (B) appliqué, 1 small heart (C) appliqué, 1 of each tulip (D, E, F, and F reverse) appliqué, 3 berry (G) appliqués, 8 flower petal (H) appliqués, and 2 flower center (I) appliqués on the cream rectangle, as shown. Use your preferred method to appliqué the shapes in place.

3. Trim the block to 23½″ × 12½″, making sure to keep the appliqué centered in the block.

ASSEMBLING THE QUILT

1. Sew the 1¼″ × 12½″ golden yellow strips to the sides of the quilt. Press the seams toward the border. Sew the 1¼″ × 25″ golden yellow strips to the top and bottom. Press.

2. Sew the 4½″ × 14″ red-and-blue strips to the sides of the quilt. Press the seams toward the newly added border. Sew the 4½″ × 33″ red-and-blue strips to the top and bottom. Press.

FINISHING

For details on sandwiching and quilting, refer to Chapter 5: Quilting by Hand and Machine (page 86). For details on binding your project, refer to Binding Your Quilt (page 114).

1. Layer and baste your quilt, and then quilt as desired. Pam machine quilted in-the-ditch around each appliquéd shape and then quilted a 1″-wide diagonal crosshatched grid over the background of the appliquéd block. The outer border was quilted in a wide rounded cable motif.

2. Sew the 2⅛″-wide blue tone-on-tone strips together end to end with diagonal seams, and use the long strip to bind the edges.

H
Cut 8.

I
Cut 2.

A
Cut 10.

G
Cut 3.

F

D

E

F
Reverse

Hearts and Flowers

C

B

Wallhanging assembly

Enlarge pattern 200%.

Wee Village Town Pillow

BY WENDY WILLIAMS

Photo by John Doughty | Spy Photography

FINISHED PILLOW: 20″ × 20″

When making an applique with felted wool, you can skip many of the traditional techniques in Preparing for Appliqué (page 60). You will not need to turn under the edges or use a seam allowance. Wool felt applique is very forgiving to work with, which makes it great for beginners! The background fabrics for this pillow are shot cotton in two shades of gray. Try using other colors or even small prints. Choose colors that allow the felt to contrast.

MATERIALS

Yardage is based on 44″-wide fabric, unless otherwise noted.

LIGHT GRAY SHOT COTTON: ¾ yard for pillow front

DARK GRAY SHOT COTTON: 1 yard
for pillow front and back

MUSLIN (OR SIMILAR): ¾ yard for backing
the appliquéd pillow front

WOOL FELT: 8–10 squares 5″ × 5″ of different colors,
including white

BLACK WOOL FELT: 1 square 10″ × 10″

GREEN WOOL FELT: 2 squares each 10″ × 10″
of 2 different greens

FUSIBLE BATTING: 20½″ × 20½″

PERLE COTTON THREAD: size 8 in a variety of colors,
including black, white, and green

PILLOW FORM: 22″ × 22″

CUTTING

LIGHT GRAY

Cut 1 square 20½″ × 20½″.

Cut 2 pieces 20½″ × 11¼″.

DARK GRAY: Cut 1 piece
10¼″ × 20½″.

MUSLIN: Cut 1 square 20½″ × 20½″.

APPLIQUÉ PIECES: Photocopy the
appliqué pattern (page 85) at 250%.
The pattern pieces also show
suggested stitching.

NOTE: *All the pieces are cut from
wool felt, so there is no need to leave
a seam allowance on the patterns.*

1. Trace the appliqué patterns onto
the dull (paper) side of freezer
paper and cut on the drawn lines.

2. Press the freezer-paper templates onto the wool felt.

3. Cut out all the appliqué pieces.

Construction

APPLIQUÉ

Note: *I like to stitch as much of the
appliqué as I can before I apply it to
the background. Refer to Preparing
for Appliqué (page 60) as needed.*

1. Stitch all the windows, roofs,
and so on to the appropriate pieces.

2. Pin the tree branches over the
tree and whipstitch them in place.

3. Stitch the leaves to the tree with
a backstitch.

Photo by John Doughty | Spy Photography

Add All the Shapes to the Background

The curved dark gray fabric is appliquéd onto the light gray fabric.

1. To create the landscape curve, place the dark gray 10¼″ × 20½″
piece right side up on top of the right side of the light gray
20½″ × 20½″ square, keeping the lower edges even. With a chalk
pencil, draw in a curved line on the dark gray piece, using the project
photo (previous page) as a guide.

2. Trim the curve of the dark gray piece, leaving a ¼″ seam allowance.
Pin and needle-turn the edge with a small running stitch close to the
folded edge. Baste the outside raw edges of the gray fabrics together.

3. Using the project photo (previous page), detail photo (page 84),
and appliqué pattern (page 85) as guides, start adding the shapes to
the background. Use appliqué pins to hold the shapes in place while
you stitch them to the background. Add flowers using small dots
of wool and colonial knots. Make the sheep faces with little chain
stitches. Add apples to the tree with small colonial knots.

4. *Optional:* Add embellishments, such as buttons and beads, for
added dimension.

FINISH

1. Fuse the fusible batting to the back side of the pillow front, following the manufacturer's instructions. Press lightly, as you don't want to flatten the felt shapes.

2. Place the muslin 20½″ × 20½″ piece against the batting side of the front, and staystitch around the outside edges. This helps stabilize the appliqué and neaten the back of the pillow top.

3. To complete the pillow, follow the instructions in Pillow Sham, Finish the Pillow, Steps 2–4 (page 152), using the 20½″ × 11¼″ light gray pieces.

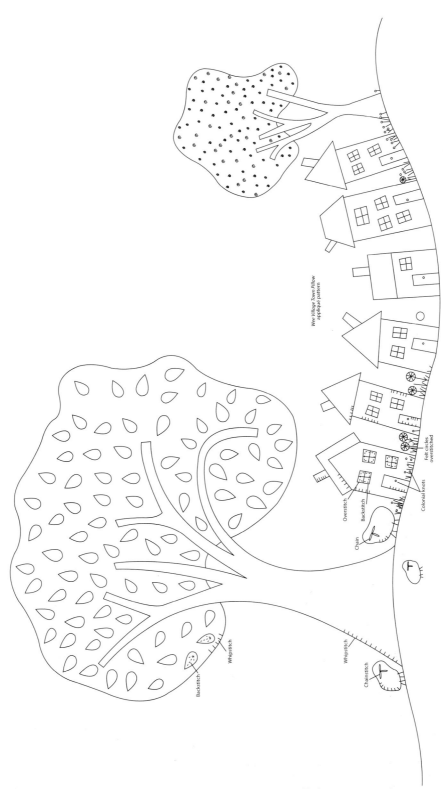

Wee Village Town Pillow
appliqué pattern

Felt circles
overstitched

Colonial knots

Overstitch

Backstitch

Chain

Whipstitch

Backstitch

Whipstitch

Chainstitch

Enlarge pattern 250%.

Chapter 5: Quilting by Hand and Machine

It's time to consider whether you're going to quilt the top by machine or hand. Your ultimate decision will be determined by the look you want to achieve and/or the intended final use (or user!) of the quilt.

Making a Quilt Sandwich

BY ELIZABETH HARTMAN

Because it takes some floor space, many of us end up doing this step in a different part of our home than we normally use for sewing. Even though I have a sewing room, I find this step always involves shuffling furniture, hauling supplies into another room, and chasing away inquisitive cats. It's worth it though, as taking the time to make a good quilt sandwich will make the next step—machine quilting—go much more smoothly!

1. Start by laying out the batting on a clean, smooth floor. Spread the quilt top on the batting, smoothing out any wrinkles. (You may need to actually crawl on top of the quilt to do this.) Trim the batting to within about 2˝ of the quilt top.

Spread the quilt top on the batting, smoothing out any wrinkles.

2. Starting at the top of the quilt, carefully roll the layered batting and quilt top into a roll.

3. Continue rolling until the batting is completely rolled up, and set it aside with the cut edge down. Don't worry about pinning the batting roll. The natural tendency of most battings is to cling to fabric, so the roll should hold itself together without any help from you.

Roll the layered batting and quilt top into a roll.

4. Now spread the quilt backing on the floor, with the right side down. Starting at the bottom of the quilt, use a strip of painter's tape to secure the edge of the quilt back to the floor. Move to the opposite (top) side and, pulling the quilt back ever so slightly toward you, tape the center top to the floor as well. Repeat with the left and right sides and each of the 4 corners, each time pulling very gently, but not stretching, to make sure the quilt back is completely smooth.

Secure the edge of the quilt back to the floor.

5. Bring back the batting roll and, starting at the bottom of the quilt back, slowly unroll the batting and quilt top onto the taped backing. You should have a few inches of leeway on all sides, but you want to make sure that (a) all parts of the quilt top are inside the edges of the quilt back and (b) the rows of blocks in the quilt top are perpendicular to the sides of the quilt back.

Unroll the batting and quilt top onto the taped backing.

tip This is your only chance to get the alignment right, so if you see that it's off, don't hesitate to reroll the batting and start over!

6. Once again, smooth out the quilt top and batting. I usually do this by starting at the bottom and crawling up the center of the quilt, smoothing as I go. You want to make things smooth, but be careful not to warp the fabric as you work. If you notice that your smoothing is making the blocks wonky, ease up a little bit and work them back into a nice gridded shape.

7. Starting in the center of the quilt and using curved safety pins, pin through all the layers (top, batting, and bottom). I recommend placing pins in a grid pattern, with a pin about every 6″. You can definitely use more pins,

Pin through all the layers.

but keep in mind that you will have to remove the pins as you quilt, so an excessive number of pins may hamper your quilting progress.

tip Placing the pins can be tricky at first, but it's something you'll probably get a feel for with practice. Let the pin do the work; just gently guide it through the layers, stopping when it touches the floor. Using too much force on the pin may distort the layers and scratch your floor. If you find opening and closing the pins to be difficult, having a pair of tweezers or needle-nose pliers on hand can be helpful.

8. Once you've finished pinning, remove the tape and trim the quilt backing to the same size as the batting.

You'll want to handle the quilt sandwich with some care. However, if you've done a good job with smoothing and pinning, you should be able to flip the sandwich over and have the back be as smooth and even as the front.

Hand Quilting

BY ALEX ANDERSON

I've always enjoyed the hand-quilting process and find that hand-quilted quilts have a special look, feel, and drape.

HAND QUILTING SUPPLIES

Needles   *Quilting needles (betweens)*—I recommend that you start with a size 8, then try a size 9, and so on. Some quilters swear by a size 12 (the smallest size), but personally, I can't thread them, and they're too fragile for me. I use a size 10.

Thread   *Quilting thread*—I generally use quilting thread, as it is a bit stronger than sewing thread. But feel free to experiment and play.

Thimble

Hoop or frame   I recommend a 16″ or 18″ quilting hoop. Do not use an embroidery hoop; it's too small and lightweight and will not hold the desired tension. As you become captivated with the process of hand quilting, you may want to invest in or build a frame.

PLACING THE QUILT IN A HOOP

When you're quilting in a hoop, the key is to keep the tension in the quilt sandwich taut but not tight. Loosen the screw of the hoop and separate the rings. Slide the smaller ring under the center of your basted quilt, and place the larger hoop (with the screw) on top of the quilt. Making sure that the top and the backing are smooth and equally stretched, clamp the rings together and partially tighten the screw.

NOTE ▶ *To avoid puckers, quilt from the center of the quilt to its outer edges.*

Press your hand down in the middle of the hooped area, while continuing to keep the layers equally stretched. This will loosen the tension just enough so that you can more easily manipulate the needle while quilting.

Remove the hoop from your quilt between quilting sessions to avoid any stretching and distortion that may occur by leaving the quilt in the hoop for an extended period of time.

THE QUILTING (ROCKING) STITCH

Although it may *look* just like a simple running stitch, the quilting stitch is unlike any other sewing stitch. This unique stitch is called the *rocking stitch* and is created using a rocking motion while the thimble pushes the needle through all three layers of the quilt. This motion requires three important fingers on your two hands working in unison. On the top of the quilt (using your dominant hand, or the hand you write with), you will use your thimble finger and thumb. Under the quilt, you will use either the pointer finger or middle finger of your other hand. All three fingers work together to manipulate the needle through the hills and valleys that your fingers create.

You'll need to identify the finger you want to wear the thimble on. I wear the thimble on my pointer finger. Many quilters prefer their middle finger. Either is fine. Try both to see which one feels the most comfortable. (Refer to Thimble on Middle or Pointer Finger, page 90, and Thimble on Thumb, page 91.)

Your next decision is whether you plan to use the end or the side of the thimble to push the needle. I find that most middle-finger quilters use the end of the thimble, while pointer-finger quilters (like me) prefer to work off the side. Again, experiment to see what works best for you.

Your early stitches will most likely feel a bit awkward at first. Stick with it! With a little practice and patience, the rocking stitch will become second nature—kind of like riding a bike.

PREPARING TO STITCH

Thread has a wrap, just like a rope. Threading your needle while the thread is still on the spool keeps the wrap of the thread going in the right direction. This results in less tangling.

Thread the needle with a single strand of thread, no longer than 18˝. Once the needle is threaded, snip the thread free of the spool. Make a knot at the end of the snipped thread.

THE QUILTER'S KNOT

This is a very simple knot that is wonderful for many sewing situations. Easy to master and easy to hide.

1. Hold the threaded needle in one hand and the tail in the other. Make a circle with the thread at the end closest to the spool, crossing the top thread over the bottom thread. Pinch it together with your forefinger and thumb.

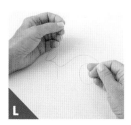 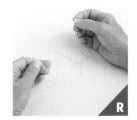

2. Slip the needle under the circle and come up through the circle.

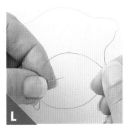 

3. Pull both tails of the circle to make the knot.

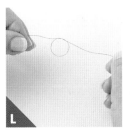 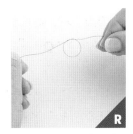

4. Insert the threaded needle into the quilt top and batting (not the backing) an inch away from the point at which you want to start quilting. Bring the needle up at the spot you plan to start stitching. Gently tug the thread until the knot "pops" in between the layers. This is called *burying the knot.*

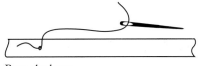

Bury the knot.

5. Put the hand without the thimble under the quilt, positioning your pointer or middle finger—whichever is more comfortable—where you will be taking the first stitch.

THIMBLE ON MIDDLE OR POINTER FINGER

1. Place your hand with the thimble on top of the quilt. Hold the needle straight up and down …

… between your thumb and ring finger (*if thimble is on middle finger*).

or

… between your thumb and middle finger (*if thimble is on pointer finger*).

With the hand in the "C" position, insert the needle straight down into the quilt where the hill has been created by your finger underneath.

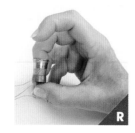

2. Release your fingers from the needle.

3. When you feel the prick of the needle on your finger below the fabric, you'll do 2 things at once. Using a dimple of the thimble to control the needle, pivot the needle tip back up through the layers. At the same time, press down with your thumb in front of the hill where the stitch is about to be made. (The needle should now be flat against the

quilt.) This forces the tip of the needle through the top of the hill, creating the first stitch.

4. As soon as you see the tip of the needle come through the hill, move the finger that is under the quilt away. Pivot the blunt end of the needle back up so that it is perpendicular to the quilt, forcing the tip down into the valley. This needle motion is about a 90° movement. As soon as you feel the tip of the needle lightly prick your finger under the quilt, repeat the process, gathering 2 or 3 stitches at a time on to your needle. Then pull on the needle and thread to draw the thread taut and complete the stitches.

tip With experience, you'll be able to get more than 2 or 3 stitches on the needle, but try not to load more than half your needle. If you do, the needle might get stuck in the quilt, slowing down the entire process. You'll also want to limit yourself to 2 or 3 stitches per needle when your stitching motifs involve lots of curves, such as feathers or grapes.

Sometimes, particularly if you're quilting in a frame, you'll want to stitch away from yourself. To do this, you'll need to control the needle with your thumb, rather than your pointer or middle finger.

Many people prefer this method because the thumb is a much stronger finger. The result is faster stitching. Also, if your hand tires, it's nice to get relief by stitching in another direction. As an added bonus, you'll find quilting feathers and grapes a snap.

You'll need a larger thimble that fits comfortably on your thumb. You will use the side of the thimble to control the needle, not the end. At first, it might seem a bit awkward to handle the needle with a thimble on your thumb, but you'll be amazed at how quickly you get used to it.

1. Hold the needle straight up and down between the thimble finger and your pointer and middle fingers. Insert the needle into the quilt top straight up and down, lightly pricking your finger underneath.

2. As soon as you feel the tip of the needle prick the underneath finger, roll the thimble to the top of the needle.

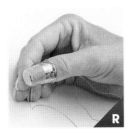

3. Rock the blunt end back, forcing the needle parallel to the quilt. With the pointer finger on your top hand, push down in front of the hill, where you'll be taking the first stitch. Keep your hand in the "C" position.

4. As soon as you see the tip of the needle come through the hill, move the finger that is under the quilt away. Pivot the blunt end of the needle back up so that it is perpendicular to the quilt, forcing the tip down into the valley. This needle motion is about a 90° movement. As soon as you feel the tip of the needle lightly prick your finger under the quilt, repeat the process.

tip If your needle gets sticky with oxidation from sweaty fingers or humidity or if it gets bent or dull from use, throw it away.

FINISHING AND BURYING THE KNOT

As you come to the end of the thread, tie a knot
close to the quilt surface. Put the needle into the
same hole from which it emerged and then back
through the quilt top. Pull gently on the thread,
burying the knot between the layers. (Some quilters
like to take a little backstitch for extra insurance.)
Pull up the remaining tail of thread and carefully
trim the end.

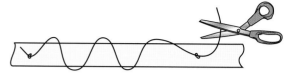

To secure your stitches, it's important to bury the knot
at the beginning and ending of your hand quilting.

tips

• Don't worry about the size of your stitches; focus
instead on consistent stitch length. Counting the
stitches on top, my first stitches were two to the inch!

• The smaller the "hill," the smaller your stitches will be.

• Don't pick out poor stitches as you go. This takes
away from valuable learning time. When the quilt is
finished, you can always go back and replace those
early stitches, but my guess is, it won't be worth your
time. In fact, you may not even be able to find them!

• You don't need to tie off the thread to move from one
section of your quilt design to another. If the distance
you need to travel is smaller than two needle lengths,
consider "walking the needle." In the direction you
want to travel, insert the needle halfway into the quilt
top, between the top and the backing. Bring the tip
of the needle halfway up through the top of the quilt.
Grab the tip of the needle and pivot the eye, which
is still between the layers. Leading with the eye of
the needle, push the needle back down into the quilt,
continuing in the desired direction. When you get to
the intended destination, push the needle up through
the top surface of the quilt and continue stitching.

Insert the needle between
layers.

Pivot the needle between
layers and push the eye
of the needle through.

• If your first stitch is always larger than the rest, try
tilting the needle forward just a bit, rather than
inserting it straight up and down. Another option
is to take a backstitch to "cheat" the look.

Tilt the needle forward
slightly.

Take a backstitch.

Machine Quilting

BY ELIZABETH HARTMAN

Machine quilting at home can be an economical, personal, and fun way to finish your quilts.

SOME GENERAL TIPS

- Always start each new project with a new needle. I recommend a 90/14 universal or quilting needle.

- Use high-quality thread. Most quilters prefer 100% cotton, but today's 100% polyester threads also work well for machine quilting. Avoid poly/cotton blends or hand quilting thread, which has a waxy coating that's incompatible with machines.

- Quilting uses a lot of thread! Wind a few extra bobbins before you start.

- Stock your quilting area with a seam ripper, thread snips, and a container for collecting your basting pins as you remove them.

- Engage your machine's needle-down function (or get in the habit of using the hand wheel to manually put your needle down whenever you stop). This will hold your place when you stop, ensuring that your rows of stitching stay straight.

- The weight of your quilt hanging off the table or into your lap can work against what your sewing machine is trying to do. Make things easier by keeping the entire quilt on the tabletop while you work. Rest the quilt on your chest or even over your shoulders rather than letting it drop down into your lap.

- Machine quilting can be physically strenuous. Take breaks to relax your arms, shoulders, and neck.

- If it's been more than a year since your machine's last tune-up, it may be a good idea to have it serviced before you attempt to machine quilt.

- Machine quilting creates lots of lint. Consult your machine's manual for instructions on how to clean your machine properly. Then get in the habit of cleaning it after you finish each quilting project.

STRAIGHT-LINE QUILTING

The feed dogs on your sewing machine are like little teeth that cycle up and down under the fabric, pulling it through the machine. This works well when you're sewing through just one or two layers of fabric, but something as thick as a quilt needs a little more help. A walking foot (sometimes called an even-feed foot) adds a second set of feed dogs on top of the fabric. With feeds dogs on both the top and the bottom, your machine can sew through a quilt sandwich with ease.

tips for success

- Follow the manufacturer's directions to install the walking foot. Most walking feet have a bar or claw that needs to be fitted above or around the needle screw.

- Test the tension and stitch length on a practice quilt sandwich. You may find that slightly increasing both the stitch length and the tension results in a nicer-looking stitch.

- Start at or near the middle of your quilt. For instance, if you're sewing parallel lines across the quilt, start with a line through the center and work your way out to the sides, alternating the direction of each row of stitching.

- Moderate your speed. Big, clunky walking feet are fabulous tools, but they're not built to move as quickly as other feet. Using a walking foot at a very high speed can result in ugly stitches and possible damage to the foot itself.

- Avoid stitching in-the-ditch, or right on the seamline. Stitching ¼˝ away from the seams rather than right on top of them looks more polished—and is much easier to do!

Straight-Line Quilting Gallery

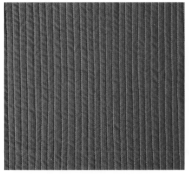

Stitching **parallel lines** about ½˝ apart produces a simple quilted look and beautiful texture. Don't worry if your lines aren't perfectly straight. That's part of the charm.

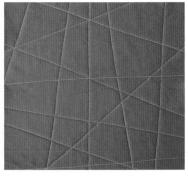

Use a piece of blue painter's tape to randomly mark a line across your quilt. Sew along the line, reposition the tape, and repeat to create a series of **crisscrossing random lines** across the quilt top.

Stopping and pivoting to make **clusters of small boxes** can be a fun way to quilt a smaller project.

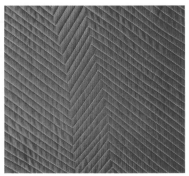

Stitching a simple shape, such as this chevron, and then **echoing** it on both sides can produce striking results.

Free-Motion Quilting

BY ELIZABETH HARTMAN

Most sewing-machine operations rely on the feed dogs pulling fabric through the machine to create uniform stitches. For free-motion quilting, however, you lower or otherwise disengage the feed dogs, which allows you to control the shape and size of the stitches and makes it possible for you to stitch in any direction. Lowering the feed dogs frees you to use the darning foot (sometimes called a free-motion quilting or embroidery foot) to draw circles, loops, or anything else you want on your quilt.

tips for success

- Free-motion quilting tends to be most successful at higher speeds. That doesn't mean you have to go as fast as you can—just fast enough to achieve smooth, fluid results.

- The key to free-motion quilting is striking a balance between the machine's speed (affected by pressure on the pedal) and the speed at which you move the quilt sandwich. If your stitches are too long, it usually means you're moving your quilt too quickly or with jerky motions. If your stitches are too small, it usually means you're not moving the quilt fast enough.

- Because you're not using the feed dogs, it's not necessary to push the quilt away from you as you

work. In fact, I find it easier to pull the quilt *toward* me, because that makes it easy to see the work that I've just done.

- Tension problems aren't always obvious from the top. Check the back of your quilt frequently to make sure everything looks right. If the bobbin thread on the back of your quilt appears to be pulled into a straight line, try increasing the thread tension.

- I find that grabbing handfuls of the quilt sandwich makes it easier for me to move the whole thing around. Other people prefer to guide the quilt with their fingertips. Experiment with different grips to find what works best for you.

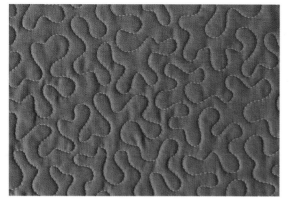

This **curved, meandering stitch** creates a beautiful texture that's accentuated when the quilt is washed.

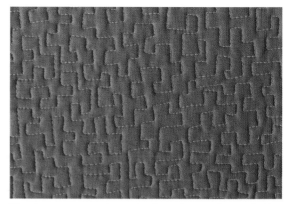

Turning curves into **boxes** lends a whimsical, retro look.

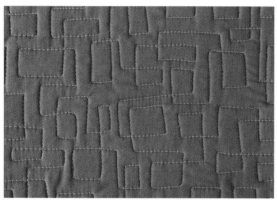

Wonky boxes with crisscrossing lines impart a modern crosshatched look.

A **meandering lightning rod** pattern complements bold fabrics.

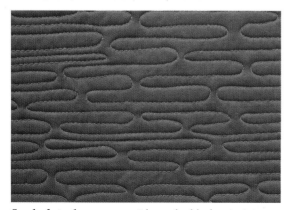

Stacked ripples contrast with regular blocky piecing.

Drawing a 2″ grid on the quilt top takes time, but it makes it easy to quilt patterns repeated in each square, such as this **dogwood flower**.

FREE-MOTION QUILTING SUPPLIES

BY CHRISTINA CAMELI

The good news is you probably already have most of the items you need for free-motion quilting: a machine, needles, and thread. Just gather a few more supplies and you'll be on your way!

Darning Foot

Unlike other sewing you've done, free-motion quilting relies on *you* to move the fabric in the direction you want it to go, instead of having the machine do so. To allow free movement of your work, you need a darning foot, sometimes called a free-motion foot. This special sewing machine foot lets you move fabric in any direction between stitches, but keeps the fabric against the stitch plate when the needle is down to allow the stitch to form properly. Plastic or metal, square or round, closed or open, they all do the same job. Any darning foot that fits your machine should work. If you have more than one darning foot to choose from, choose the one that offers you better visibility. In other words, an open toe rather than a closed toe, offset shank versus inline, thinner versus thicker. Your local sewing machine dealer can help you find a darning foot that will fit your machine.

Variety of darning feet

A Clean Machine

During sewing, and particularly quilting, lint from the thread, the fabrics, and the batting will accumulate around the foot and under the stitch plate. Lint buildup can interfere with the action of the thread enough to cause thread breakage or skipped stitches. If you've never cleaned out your machine before, now is the time to learn.

CLEANING A SEWING MACHINE

Remove the bobbin and clean out the inside of the bobbin case. Lint in the corners of the bobbin case and housing can cause problems. Give a quick wipe to this area with every bobbin change.

Remove bobbin to clean out bobbin case and housing.

Next, remove the stitch plate (if it can be removed), using the owner's manual to guide you. This is usually done by releasing a lever or loosening screws. Use a soft brush or a scrap of batting to wipe away any clumps of lint accumulating around the feed dogs and bobbin housing. Do this full, plate-off cleanout every three or four bobbin changes. Oil the machine regularly as recommended in the owner's manual.

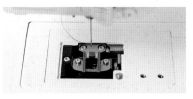

Stitch plate removed for cleaning

tip Cut batting scraps into 2″ squares to use for lint cleanup.

Machine's Extension Table

Many sewing machines have a free arm for detail sewing and a larger extension table that fits around the free arm. Trying to quilt on a skinny free arm is an exercise in frustration. If your machine doesn't have an extension table, try this test: Place your hands as shown in the picture below. If your palms and fingers are not supported, you'll need to put a table around the machine bed.

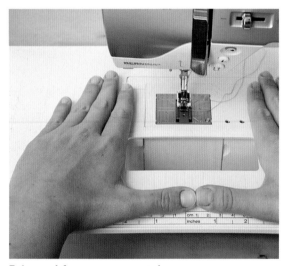

Palms and fingers are supported.

If you need an extension table, you can order a custom Plexiglas extension table through your local sewing machine store. Alternatively, you can purchase a sewing table that a machine lowers into, so that the tabletop lies flush with the surface of the sewing machine. This creates a continuous flat surface and reduces the effort necessary to move the quilt top as you stitch.

Sewing machine extension table

Feed Dogs Adjustment

When a sewing machine moves the fabric for straight stitching, it does so with the feed dogs, which pull the fabric forward with every stitch. For free-motion stitching, you must stop the feed dogs from pulling on the fabric, so that you can guide the work in the direction you want it to go. If your machine has a lever or switch to lower the feed dogs, use it and you can move fabric freely. If not, there are other ways you can stop the feed dogs from interfering.

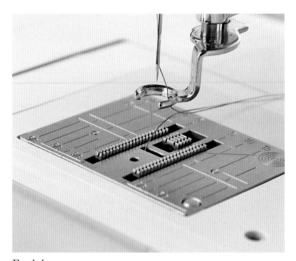

Feed dogs up

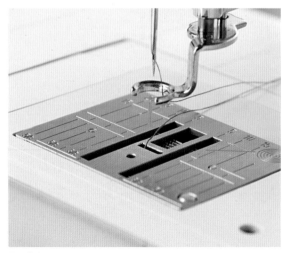

Feed dogs down

The simplest solution is simply setting the machine's stitch length to zero. At this setting, the feed dogs will go up and down, but they will not pull on the fabric. Some quilters prefer to stitch this way, even though their machines are able to lower the feed dogs. So if you can't lower the feed dogs on your machine, don't fret; just set the stitch length to zero!

If you prefer that the feed dogs not touch the fabric at all, you may cover them with an index card. Punch a hole in the middle for the needle to pass through. Tape all four edges of the index card to the machine to keep them from catching on your work. Instead of an index card, you may wish to try a specialty mat for free-motion quilting that adheres to the machine bed, covering the feed dogs while providing a smooth, slick surface to allow easy movement of the quilt.

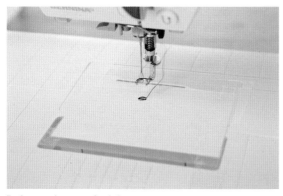

Index card covers feed dogs.

Alternatively, your machine may have a lever to raise the stitch plate above the feed dogs. I typically recommend against this approach because it will take up valuable space between the stitch plate and the darning foot, squishing the fabric and making it harder to move your work.

As another option, you may be able to purchase a feed dog cover for your machine that will snap to the stitch plate over the feed dogs. Experiment and see what works best for you.

Needles

Old needles don't work well for free-motion quilting. A dull or slightly bent needle will soon result in skipped stitches or broken threads. Start quilting with a nice sharp needle. Most machines will work well with either universal needles or quilting needles. Quilting needles are a little sharper than universal needles.

Some needles that can be used for free-motion quilting

The numbers on the needle package refer to the size of the needle in the sizing systems of Europe and the United States. The larger the number, the larger the size of the needle and its eye. Use larger needles for thicker threads. I recommend universal 80/12 or quilting 90/14 needles to start.

Replace needles after about 8 hours of stitching, or when thread or stitch problems tell you to do so. Sometimes a different size or type of needle is called for to deal with a specific machine problem.

Many threads work well for free-motion quilting. Cotton, polyester, and silk in a variety of thicknesses are commonly used. Thread thickness is frequently described using a weight system. The larger the number of the thread weight, the *thinner* the thread, and the subtler the stitching will appear. The smaller the number, the *thicker* the thread, and the more visible each stitch will be. Most of the projects in this book were stitched with 40- and 50-weight threads.

Aurifil 28/2 cotton

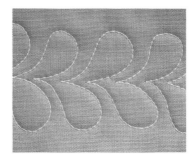

Aurifil 40/2 cotton

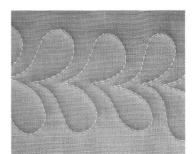

So Fine 50/3 polyester

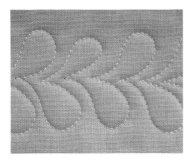

The Bottom Line 60/2 polyester

YLI silk #100 2-ply

Some threads that can be used for free-motion quilting

tip Thread weights are often given along with the number of yarns in the thread. For example, a 40-weight, 3-ply thread is generally indicated as 40/3. Some quilting threads, however, are described with a number sign (#) before the number. This is not always the same as the thread weight. The best way to understand how a thread will appear on a quilt is to stitch a test sample.

It is fine to start with whatever thread you have at home. However, free-motion stitching puts a lot of stress on thread, so threads that you normally use may not perform as well as you expect under these circumstances. Try new threads if you encounter problems or get curious. Over time and with experimentation, you'll eventually land on a favorite thread for both your stitching style and your machine's particular temperament. I have great luck with both Aurifil and Superior threads for their strength and the minimal lint they produce while quilting.

For most projects, I recommend using the same thread in the top and bobbin. Some machines work best when the top and bobbin threads are the same weight. However, many quilters use different threads in the top and bobbin without difficulty. Some quilters prefer to use a very fine specialty thread in the bobbin.

Fabric

Quilting-weight cottons and linen are used for most of the projects in this book. If you are just starting free-motion quilting, try to avoid fabrics such as denim or batiks, which can present special challenges. If you do use batiks, be sure to prewash them to remove any residual wax from the fabric.

Batting

For quilts and quilted projects, the choice of batting will affect the free-motion quilting results. In general, low-loft battings are ideal for free-motion quilting. Cotton, polyester, wool, bamboo, and silk are all used with success by free-motion quilters. Avoid any batting you could describe as puffy.

Low-loft battings

Basting Pins

To hold quilt layers together and keep them from shifting and puckering as you quilt, you should temporarily baste them together. I baste my work with curved basting pins, which are widely available and can be reused. Some quilters prefer to spray baste their quilts, and this method typically works just fine for free-motion quilting. Feel free to try this approach.

Curved basting pins

Quilting Gloves

Quilting gloves are available in different sizes and have a textured surface to increase traction on fabric. They give you better control over the quilt than bare hands and keep your hands from becoming fatigued as quickly. Gloves are a small investment and will last for years. My favorites have small grippy dots on them that provide traction on both the palms and the fingers. Some quilters cut off one or two fingertips of their gloves to make needle threading and pin removal easier.

Gloves for quilting

As alternatives to quilting gloves, some quilters prefer latex gloves, gardening gloves, industrial glove liners, or rubber office fingertips. Others prefer to grasp their quilts with well-moisturized bare hands. I encourage new quilters to start with quilting gloves but try alternatives if they feel uncomfortable with the hold they have on the quilt.

Sketches

In a way, free-motion quilting is drawing with thread. Sketching, therefore, is a great way to practice. I recommend dedicating a big blank journal for sketching quilting designs. Use this journal to get you used to creating continuous-line designs. Put the pen down and see what patterns you can create without lifting the pen from the page. Try variations on a theme. How many designs can you doodle with spirals in them, for example?

When you have a project to stitch, let your journal help you. Before quilting a new design, fill a few pages of the journal with it. Working on paper helps you get a feel for how the design flows and where the twists and turns come. It's much cheaper and easier to work these things out on paper than on fabric.

Some quilters prefer to save paper by practicing their sketches on a dry erase board. Others use old phone books and markers. Some doodle

during meetings on bits of scrap paper—whatever works for you. Don't underestimate the benefit of sketching for improving eye-hand coordination and familiarity with quilting designs.

tip Sketch new designs in your journal whenever they present themselves, and the journal will soon become an invaluable design library in addition to being a tool for experimentation and practice.

BY CHRISTINA CAMELI

Sitting down to stitch for the first time is embarking on a journey. Free-motion quilting asks a bit more of you and your machine than typical sewing. Take challenges a step at a time and get to know your sewing machine better than you ever have before.

START-UP CHECKLIST

Go through this checklist each time you start quilting.

• Clean machine

• Extension table

• Darning foot

• Fresh needle

• Feed dogs down or covered (*optional*)

• Quilting thread

• Quilting gloves

• Set machine for straight stitch

• Adjust the machine stitch length and width to zero (or as low as they will go).

Now let's start quilting!

Making a Practice Pad

Before you start stitching on a project, do some warm-up stitching on a practice pad. Cut two pieces of fabric and a piece of batting to create a mini quilt sandwich about 12″ × 18″. Baste it with pins about every 5″.

Getting a Hold on the Quilt

I have experimented with different quilt holds, and the one I always come back to is the U shape. This hold allows me to move the quilt with precision and keeps puckers from developing as I stitch.

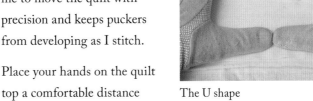

The U shape

Place your hands on the quilt top a comfortable distance apart, with your thumbs extended toward each other, so that the thumbs and forefingers create a U shape. The tips of your fingers and thumbs rest on the quilt, as well as the outside edge of the palms. The rest of the palm is lifted somewhat off the quilt top, in a relaxed position. This creates much less hand stress than trying to keep the entire hand flat on the quilt. Use a slight downward and outward pressure with your hands to keep the area you are stitching flat, preventing wrinkles. While a number of quilting hoops are marketed to free-motion quilters, I think no quilting hoop is more adaptable or easier to use than your own hands!

Keep your hands closer in for intricate work and place them farther out when quilting larger designs. You will have good control of the quilt within the U, but control will deteriorate as you stitch outside its boundaries. Stop and reposition your hands as you go, keeping the needle within the U.

tip Some quilters prefer grabbing their quilts with one or both hands. Feel free to try different holds on the quilt if the U is not working for you.

1. Place the quilt under the machine and lower the presser foot.

2. Take a stitch into the quilt and then bring the needle back up to its highest point.

3. Tug lightly on the tail of the top thread until you can see a loop of the bobbin thread come up through the quilt. Pull this loop gently until you have brought the entire tail of the bobbin thread up to the top.

Pulling thread loop up

4. Reposition so the needle is directly over the place where you took the first stitch.

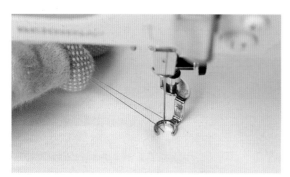

Needle repositioned

5. Place one hand on the quilt. Hold the thread tails back with the other hand. Lock the first stitches by taking a few tiny stitches forward and backward over one another. You are securing the threads in place to keep them from unraveling over time. If you prefer, you can just take a few stitches in place to secure the threads.

Locking the stitches

6. Place your hands on the quilt in the U shape and begin stitching the design. Guide the quilt with your hands while you press the pedal. Keep your hands on the quilt in the U shape. Trim the thread ends as needed to keep from stitching over them.

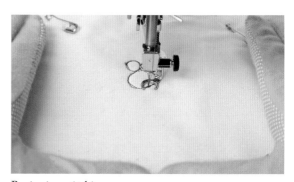

Beginning stitching

7. When the stitching needs to go beyond the U, stop stitching and reposition your hands.

Stitching has reached edge of U.

Hands repositioned.

Some machines have a needle-down feature that stops the needle in the down position. This makes repositioning faster; if the needle is down in the fabric you are free to reposition your hands without worrying that the quilt will shift. If the needle stops in the up position, move your hands one at a time to keep the quilt in place while you reposition your hands. Or use the hand wheel to put the needle down so that you are free to remove both hands from the quilt.

8. If you have a basting pin within the U, remove it when you reposition your hands; then you are free to stitch within the entire area.

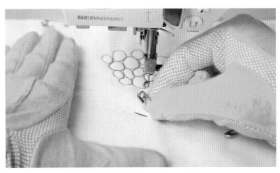

Remove basting pins as you come to them.

9. Continue in this way: Stitch, reposition, stitch. Readjust the quilt as needed so it does not catch on the corners of the table.

10. When you are ready to stop, lock the stitches as you did at the beginning, by taking a few small stitches back and forth over one another. Pull the quilt out and clip the threads close to the quilt top.

tip Starts and stops are not as secure as continuous stitching, so try to plan the quilting for as few stops and starts as possible.

Tension Adjustment

The top and bobbin threads each have adjustable tension. The tension of one thread affects the other thread's behavior. If the tension is out of balance, you will see one thread being pulled to the other side by the thread with the higher tension. Tension may need adjustment depending on the thickness of the item you are stitching and the thickness of the threads being used.

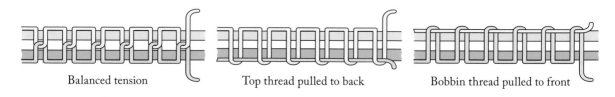

Balanced tension   Top thread pulled to back   Bobbin thread pulled to front

······················· **How should you adjust the tension?** ·······················

If the top thread is being pulled to the back …

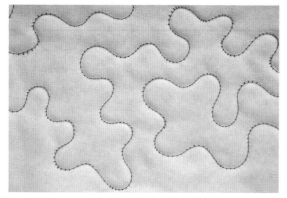

Top (red) thread being pulled to back. Bobbin thread is not being pulled into quilt sandwich; it is just lying on back of quilt.

Increase the top thread tension (turn dial to the right, or to a higher number if the tension dial uses numbers) or decrease the bobbin thread tension (turn the bobbin tension screw counterclockwise).

If the bobbin thread is being pulled to the top …

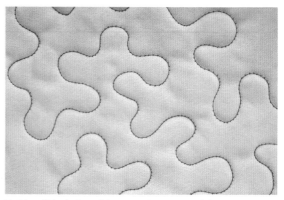

Bobbin (blue) thread being pulled to top. Top thread is not being pulled into quilt sandwich; it is just lying on top of quilt.

Decrease the top thread tension (turn dial to the left, or to a lower number if the tension dial uses numbers) or increase the bobbin thread tension (turn the bobbin tension screw clockwise).

Most of the time, only the top thread tension will need adjustment. However, I sometimes encounter machines whose bobbin tension needs adjusting as well. You are qualified to do this! Use the sewing machine manual to identify the bobbin tension adjustment screw. Mark the original setting of the screw by making a dot with a permanent marker, so you can return the tension screw to its original setting if needed. Make only a small turn at a time, equivalent to five minutes if the screw were the face of a clock. Test on a practice pad after each adjustment until you have solved the problem.

Longarm Machine Quilting

BY ANGELA WALTERS

LONGARM SUPPLIES

Don't be tricked into thinking you need a longarm quilting machine to machine quilt your own quilts. While it does make quilting easier, it definitely isn't a necessity. Most free-motion designs can be quilted using a domestic sewing machine (DSM) or a longarm.

The same goes for all the available add-ons. For instance, I quilt on a Gammill longarm, but it is the smallest longarm available. It doesn't have a stitch regulator or a needle up-and-down function. All it has is a speed control and an on–off switch. And that is just fine for me!

Marking Tools for Longarm Machine Quilting

A variety of marking tools will make quilting easier.

Some people think that free-motion quilting means that you don't use markings of any kind. This is incorrect. Free-motion quilting refers to the fact that the quilting is hand guided. Using stencils and marking tools will help keep the designs consistent. It is my belief that every quilter, whether a longarmer or those using a DSM, should have an assortment of marking tools.

All my quilting is free-motion, but sometimes I mark larger motifs on the quilt. I also use registration marks on my quilt. These marks help me ensure that designs are consistent. These are a few of my favorite marking tools:

Water-soluble pens I will admit that I am a snob when it comes to water-soluble pens. I use only Dritz blue marking pens. I have never had a problem with the marks not coming out, so I figure, why try anything else? I am very cautious to remove the marks quickly, using only cold water, following the manufacturer's instructions.

Chalk Chalk is a great way to mark dark fabrics or quilts that I don't want to get wet. Chalk pencils and chalk sticks are great for this purpose.

Stencils Stencils are great for quickly marking designs on a quilt. The stencils I use most often are grids for marking registration lines. The registration lines help me keep my designs even. I use a chalk pounce pad to mark the stencils. The pad holds blue or white chalk and can be rubbed over the stencil to quickly mark the design. Stencils are available in all different shapes and sizes.

tip When choosing stencils, make sure they are *continuous line* or *machine-quilting* stencils. Hand-quilting stencils have too many starts and stops and will be frustrating.

Rulers If you are quilting on a longarm quilting machine, make sure you have a good-quality ruler. I use a 2″ × 12″ acrylic ruler. It is great for marking lines and for guiding the machine along straight lines and seams.

Notions Don't forget the little things such as pins, scissors, and extra needles.

MY TIPS FOR FREE-MOTION QUILTERS

BY ANGELA WALTERS

DRAW, DRAW, DRAW

I love to say that 80% of quilting is knowing where to go next. (Surely there is a mathematical algorithm to prove this.) When asked how to get better at quilting, I always tell quilters to practice drawing the designs over and over on paper until they are comfortable with the design. Draw a box and fill it with the design you are practicing. By doing this, you will learn how to fill the space evenly and how not to get yourself stuck in a corner.

DON'T BE TOO HARD ON YOURSELF

When your nose is 2″ from the quilt top, you can see every little imperfection. Remember that every little mistake adds character, and you probably won't notice it from a few feet away. When you are finished with the quilt, put it away for a day. When you pull it out the next day, set it across the room and admire it from afar. Chances are, it will look great.

PRACTICE MAKES PERFECT

Anything worth doing well takes a lot of practice. One common misconception is that some people instantly know how to machine quilt. But you can ask accomplished machine quilters and they will tell you that it takes a lot of time and practice. So don't get discouraged; keep practicing, and you will get the hang of it.

LONGARM QUILTING TIPS

BY GINA PERKES

Backing Fabric Selection

Never underestimate the power of the backing fabric. When I was a fairly new longarm quilter, quilting for hire, I would cringe when my clients would deliver their quilts to me with white sheets selected as their backing fabric. As icing on the cake, they usually preferred that I use dark threads for these particular scenarios. You might wonder why this frightened me so. Well, have you ever heard the phrase "sticks out like a sore thumb"? I was, and probably still am, simply not confident in my ability to quilt an entire piece without a "sore thumb" (mistake). We can use every precaution and check the underside often, yet an occasional loop or tension faux pas may still present itself.

BUSY PRINTS

Busily patterned prints are a great choice for concealing the underside of your work. As a basis for determining the right backing fabric color, consider the thread color(s) that you are likely to use on the top. Because the bobbin and top threads should be similar in color, I like to match my backing and bobbin colors closely. When I plan to incorporate many different thread colors, I will select a backing fabric combining colors similar to those of my planned threads.

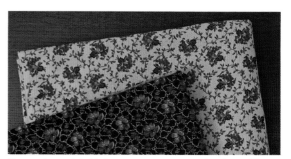

Busy prints with high contrast are a great backing fabric choice.

BACKING WEAVE

When selecting backing fabric, also consider thread count. Fabrics that have a softer hand and are more loosely woven are less likely to form aggravating puckers. Puckers are a quilter's bad dream; folds are a quilter's nightmare. They always seem to remain unnoticed until they have been trapped by hundreds of yards of quilting. One interesting quality about little stitches: What takes minutes to put in takes hours to take out. Because of this, I have decided that it is best to take every precaution to avoid puckered disasters.

tip Prewashing your backing fabrics in warm water also will help prevent puckering because it removes the sizing and loosens up the fibers a bit.

Backing Preparation

It is very important that your backing fabric is cut squarely. A squared-up backing will roll up evenly onto the machine, reducing the emergence of puckers and folds. Don't rely on the fabric shop to cut your fabric straight. Fabric is often wound onto the bolt less than perfectly, resulting in imperfect or angled cuts. I always buy generous amounts of my selected backing fabric. Several inches may need to be removed to create a squared piece. In addition, you should always allow at least 5″ excess along both sides, the top, and the bottom. If the backing requires combined pieces to meet the size requirement, seam the pieces and then square it up as one.

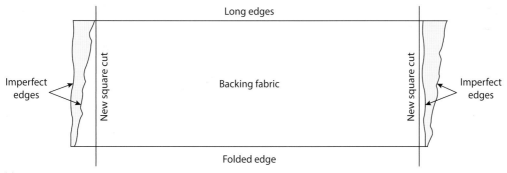

To square up the backing fabric, fold the 2 long edges together and then make clean 90° cuts at both ends.

Quilt Loading

Quilt loading is the final step before the real fun begins. I pin my quilts directly to the machine's canvas leaders. Zippered leaders are a great option if you plan to remove the quilt from the machine prior to its completion, in the case of sharing the machine or alternating work. I used to share a machine with my mom, and we would use zippered leaders to accommodate one another. Nowadays, I focus my attention on one quilt at a time, so I don't find it necessary to use zippered leaders. The preparation time involved in applying the zippered leaders to the quilt is equal to the pinning time, so I choose to eliminate the extra step. It is easy to get eager as the quilting process draws near, but don't cut corners at this point—proper quilt loading will reduce bumps in the quilting road ahead. Most often, I pin the longest edges to the machine to reduce rolling time.

tip The machine's canvas leaders should come premarked at the centers. I add additional measurements to my leaders from the centers out. This extra step is a precautionary measure that helps to maintain a squared-up quilt.

Numbered markings can help keep a quilt squared up.

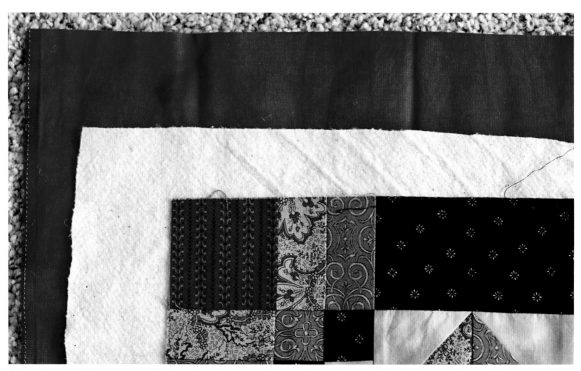

Always lay the 3 layers out on the floor (or other large, flat area) in order—backing, batting, quilt top. Make certain that you have allowed an excess of at least 5″ per edge on both the batting and the backing pieces.

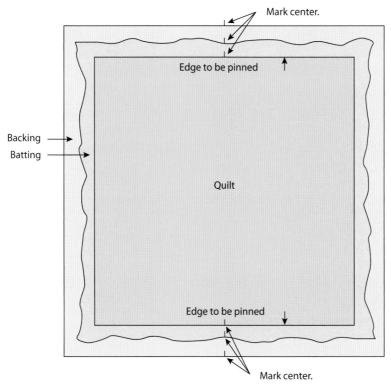

Mark center.

Edge to be pinned

Backing

Batting

Quilt

Edge to be pinned

Mark center.

Note the measurements of the edges you plan to pin.
Mark the centers of the to-be-pinned edges for all 3 layers.

Pin the 3 layers of the upper edge to the leader, matching the center marks and outer edge measurements. If you would like additional space at the upper edge for easier stitching or binding applications, simply drop the edge of the quilt down a few inches and then pin or baste.

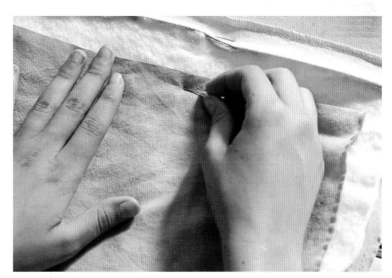

If you would like extra space, drop the top down from the backing and batting layers, and then pin or baste it in place.

Flip the quilt top and batting to the back so you can focus on loading and rolling the backing fabric accurately. Pin the bottom edge of the backing fabric to the backing leader, matching the centers and outer edge markings. Now that both upper and lower edges are pinned, you are ready to begin rolling. Let the loose backing fabric hang between the bars—it may touch the floor. Roll slowly, keeping the fabric straight and smoothing often to prevent wrinkles from developing. Keep the width of the fabric taut so the edges line up evenly after each advancement of the rolling process.

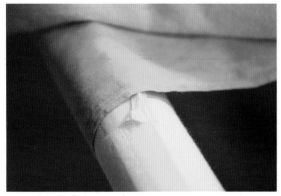

The edges of the backing fabric should line up evenly as you roll.

tip It is important that the floor beneath your machine be cleaned often to prevent objects from clinging to the batting or backing as the fabric brushes the floor. I use a new toilet brush to collect stray threads from my carpet, and then I run the vacuum to prevent unwanted debris from making its way into my quilt. I once stitched a small leaf into a quilt accidentally. The leaf remains to this day, adding a bit of texture to the piece and serving as a reminder to keep things tidy.

Spread the batting over the taut backing fabric evenly. This is a good time to check for clinging threads or other objects that could become trapped in the quilting.

Pin the remaining edge of the quilt top to the leader, matching the centers and outer edge markings. Roll the edge up slowly, as with the backing, keeping it smooth and wrinkle-free. Keep the edges even as you roll the quilt up.

tip When rolled up, the layers should be snug but have some shock absorbency. If you drop your scissors on the quilt and they launch across the room, it's a good indication that the quilt layers are rolled too tightly.

Basted Temporary Border

If the edges of a quilt are critical, as with pieced borders, you can create some breathing room by basting a temporary muslin border along the edges. This enables you to stitch very close to the edge of the border without distorting the shape or hitting obstacles (clamps, pins, runners, and so on). Also, this piece can serve as a practice space or for last-minute tension checks.

Cover up the dangerous row of pins.

"How do you handle your stops and starts?"
This might be the most frequently asked question in my classes. It is with confidence that I can share my techniques with you. I can assure you with the utmost honesty, I have never received a bad grade from a quilt show judge in this subject. We all desire a quilt that is visually pleasing, but the quilt's strength and life expectancy are also important. Once we place the intended stitches in our quilt, we expect them to stay. Here are a couple of methods for you to try.

Tiny stitches   This is the method I use most often. It is a good choice for most of the thread weights you will likely be using. Simply take three tiny stitches prior to takeoff using the single-stitch button, and then proceed. When you come to the end of the quilting path, stop. Take three tiny stitches, again with the single-stitch button, and then clip the thread. Trust me; those threads aren't going to escape. Have you ever made a mistake where small stitches were involved and then tried to remove them? It is not easy—those little stitches are stubborn and difficult to dislodge.

Buried threads   If you have selected a heavy thread weight or are stitching open designs in which stops and starts will be obvious, you might choose to bury the thread ends into the layers using a hand needle. This is quite a bit more time consuming than simply taking tiny stitches, but the results are very clean. I use a self-threading hand needle to avoid the eye strain that might develop after numerous re-threads.

If you have further quilting planned for the quilt, you can secure the two thread tails (top and bobbin) by burying them in the middle of your quilt sandwich. Direct the threads toward spaces to be quilted and they will be held securely in place when that area is quilted.

If no further quilting will be done in the vicinity, you may wish to pull the thread tails to the back side and secure them with a knot, a dab of liquid seam sealant, or both. This technique is also useful when the top contains light-colored fabrics that thread tails might show through.

Chapter 6:
Quilt Finishing Techniques

Binding Your Quilt

BY ELIZABETH HARTMAN

Binding is the finishing frame around a quilt. My favorite method is straight-grain binding made from strips cut along the grain of the fabric rather than on the bias. All the quilts in this book were made with this type of binding, which is machine sewn to the front of the quilt and finished by hand on the back.

SIMPLE DOUBLE-FOLD BINDING

1. Cut binding strips along the fabric grain and trim away the selvages. Sew the strips together end to end, using ¼″ seam allowances, and press the seams open. With the wrong sides together, press the entire binding in half lengthwise.

tip Straight-grain binding, or using pieces sewn together end to end, is perfect for making patchwork or scrappy binding. That can mean inserting one or two contrasting pieces between longer strips or making the entire binding from small pieces. Experiment and have fun! Just keep in mind that additional seam allowances add bulk. The extra bulk may make it difficult to achieve perfectly mitered corners, so try to keep the seams between strips away from the corners.

2. Prepare your quilt for binding by trimming all the layers even with the quilt top and squaring up the quilt top if necessary. Start in the center of one side and pin the raw (unfolded) edge of the binding to the quilt's edge. When you reach a corner, fold the binding up at a 45° angle.

Sew the binding strips together.

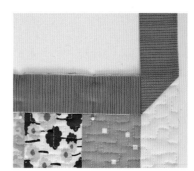

Trim all the layers even with the quilt top.

3. Fold the binding back toward the quilt, aligning the fold with the top edge to create a mitered corner.

4. Fold down the mitered corner and pin it in place.

5. Continue pinning, repeating Steps 2–4 at each corner, until you reach the point where you started. Bring together the 2 ends of the binding, fold each piece back onto itself so the ends are butting, and press in place.

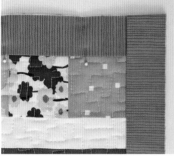

Align the fold with the top edge to create a mitered corner.

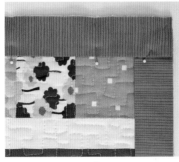

Pin the corner in place.

Bring together the 2 ends of the binding and press in place.

6. Match the creases you've just pressed and sew the ends together along the crease. Trim the seam allowance to ¼˝, press the seam open, and pin the binding back in place. You should now have continuous binding pinned all the way around your quilt sandwich.

7. Use a ¼˝ seam allowance to sew the binding to the quilt. When you come to a corner, sew up to—but not beyond—the miter. Stop stitching and trim the threads.

tip If you'd rather not use pins, feel free to sew the binding on without pinning it first. Leave about 6˝ of extra binding at your starting point. Then sew the binding to the quilt edge, folding miters at each corner, just as if you were pinning. Stop several inches from where you started and refer to Steps 5 and 6 to join the two ends of the binding.

Sew the ends together.

Sew the binding to the quilt.

8. Fold back the mitered corner. Resume your stitching at the corner, repeating Step 7 at each of the following corners until you reach the point where you started.

Continue sewing around the quilt.

9. Fold the binding to the back of the quilt—the fold you pressed into the binding earlier and the mitered corners should make this easy. Use pins or binding clips to secure a section of the binding in place.

10. To create a knotless start for hand finishing, fold a length of thread in half and thread the fold through the needle. Pull through far enough that the loose ends are near the eye of the needle and the loop is at the other end (where a knot would normally be). Pull the needle through the quilt back and batting, near the edge of the binding, leaving the end loop sticking out just a bit. Bring the needle through the edge of the binding and then back through the loop. Pull the needle until the loop closes and the thread is anchored securely.

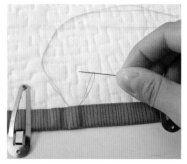

Create a knotless start for hand finishing.

11. Hand stitch the binding in place, pushing the needle through the quilt back and batting and pulling it back up through the very edge of the binding. Continue sewing, making a stitch about every ¼˝.

Hand stitch the binding in place.

12. When you reach a corner, sew right up to the quilt's edge before folding back the mitered corner and continuing onto the next side.

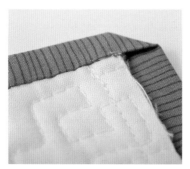

Sew up to the quilt's edge before folding back the mitered corner.

13. Continue until the binding is completely stitched in place.

Finish the binding.

tip Take good care of your finished work. Quilts made with cotton generally can be machine washed and dried. I use cool water, a gentle wash cycle, and gentle detergent, and I tumble dry on low heat. If you're concerned about colors bleeding, consider trying a color catcher product. Designed to soak up any loose dye in a wash cycle, these products are usually available where laundry soap is sold.

Adding a Hanging Sleeve

BY ALEX ANDERSON

At some point, you may wish to display your quilt on the wall. If you plan to enter your quilt in a show, be sure to carefully read the rules regarding the size and application required for the sleeve.

1. Cut a strip of fabric the width of the quilt × 8″ wide. Hem each of the short edges.

2. Fold the strip in half lengthwise, wrong sides together, and stitch. Press the seam open.

3. Position the sleeve with the long seam against the back of the quilt. Pin and whipstitch the long folded edges to the back of the quilt.

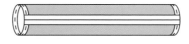

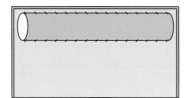

4. Apply the binding as usual. The stitching that secures the binding to the top edge of the quilt will also secure the top edge of the sleeve.

5. Pin and whipstitch the bottom edge of the sleeve to the back of the quilt.

✷ *tip* With this method, the sleeve is attached to the quilt before the binding is added.

1. Cut a strip of fabric the width of the quilt × 8″ wide. Hem each of the short edges.

2. Fold the strip in half lengthwise, wrong sides together, aligning the long raw edges.

3. Center and align the long raw edges of the sleeve with the top edge of the quilt back; machine baste using a scant ¼″.

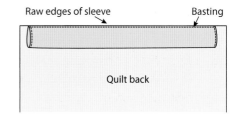

Making a Label

BY ALEX ANDERSON

The information that you include on your label will be treasured for generations to come. Use a permanent fabric pen on the back (or even the front, if the design lends itself) of the quilt, or create a beautiful patch designed especially for the quilt with hand or machine embroidery, colorful fabric pens, or fonts and photos that you print on your computer.

Special labels created by Cindy Needham

For assurance that the identifying information will not be lost (and to deter theft), some machine quilters attach the label to the quilt backing before basting so that the label is permanently affixed by the quilting. Another option is to write identifying information directly on the quilt where the label will cover it, ensuring that the info will remain even if the label itself is lost or removed.

The following information should be considered essential:

• The name of the quilt

• Your name and the name of the quilter (if different)

• Where and when the quilt was made

• You may also like to add the dimensions of the quilt—handy when you are entering the quilt in a show.

If the quilt is made for a special person or occasion, you might like to add the following:

• The name of the recipient (if the quilt is made to celebrate the birth of a child, add the child's birth date and place, the parents' names, and your relationship to the child)

• The special occasion for the quilt (such as birth, christening, graduation, wedding)

• Any additional personal sentiments

CARING FOR YOUR QUILTS

BY ALEX ANDERSON

If you have a top-loading washing machine, here's what I recommend for washing your quilts:

1. Fill the basin in your washing machine with cool water and mix in a mild soap.

2. Place the quilt in the washing machine and allow it to soak, occasionally swishing the quilt around in the water with gentle hands. *Do not* use the agitate cycle on the washing machine.

3. Allow the quilt to soak for approximately 20 minutes. Advance to the rinse cycle and give the quilt a cool-water rinse; then run a gentle spin cycle to remove the excess water.

4. Remove the quilt from the machine and air dry it flat, face down on a large light-colored towel or sheet. If it's a nice day, dry it outdoors in a spot where birds are not likely to visit.

tip If you don't have a top-loading machine or if your machine won't allow you to prefill before adding the quilt, launder your quilt the old-fashioned way by soaking it in the bathtub instead. Drain the water and press the quilt gently against the side of the tub to remove excess water (and weight!) before removing the quilt to dry.

Dry cleaning a quilt is always a risky business. If a quilt is made of materials that cannot be washed, and it's hopelessly filthy, you *might* want to risk it. Be aware, however, that it is a risk (including the possibility that the colors might run) … every time!

As for storing your quilts, the best way is unfolded on a bed—layered, if you like—and covered with a sheet to protect them from light, dust, and pets.

If you must fold your quilts, never store them in plastic bags, which can trap harmful moisture. Use clean cotton pillowcases instead. You also want to avoid direct contact with wood, as the oils can leach out into the fabric. To form a protective barrier, line shelves or trunks with clean cotton sheets, lengths of muslin, or special, acid-free paper.

Another alternative is to store your quilts rolled. A foam pool noodle makes a great core. If that's not an option, create your own noodle by crunching up a long strip of acid-free paper instead.

Roll your quilt around a foam pool noodle for storage.

Chapter 7:
Beyond the Basics

Crazy Quilting

BY JUDITH BAKER MONTANO

Four-square wallhanging, by Judith Baker Montano

Angelo Asti (1847–1907) created the first Glamour Girls. He was born in Italy but lived in Paris, France, where he painted many beautiful portraits. Later, the paintings were reproduced as postcards, which are highly prized collectibles today.

Crazy quilting is the method of sewing varied shapes of fancy fabrics to a wholecloth foundation. The fabrics form a collaged asymmetrical design. After the foundation is covered, each seam is decorated with embellishments and embroidered stitch combinations. Unlike a traditional quilt, a crazy quilt has no batting and is tacked to a wholecloth backing.

PREPARING THE FOUNDATION

Always cut the foundation larger than the actual pattern. This allows for any puckering of tight tension that could draw up the size. For example, if I am going to piece the yoke of a vest, I transfer the yoke outline onto the foundation. On this foundation, I draw the actual seamlines, but I cut out the shape ½″ larger all around. This is a principle I follow in all crazy quilt projects, from quilt squares and vest fronts to purses and pendants.

For good piecing, I never work on an area larger than a 12″ × 12″ square. On a larger foundation, the outside pieces become too wide, too long, and stripy. To prevent this, I cut large garment patterns in half for a more manageable size and better piecing.

After the foundation has been filled in, I cut down the piece to the proper size. I do this with all crazy quilt projects.

HOW MUCH FABRIC YOU'LL NEED

There is no pattern or one set way to create a crazy quilt block, so it is hard to judge the amount of fabric needed. I always plan on more fabrics than needed, and this gives me freedom of choice.

Note: *When choosing fabrics for a project, always make sure that half are patterns and half are solids. Be sure to have a good variety of textures along with shiny and matte finishes.*

- **For 1 crazy quilt block**

  Use 10–12 fabrics. For a single block, be sure to use each fabric at least twice to create design flow. With this number of fabrics you have freedom of choice.

- **For 4 crazy quilt blocks**

  Use 14–18 fabrics. Be sure to have enough of each fabric so it can be used twice in each block. Make sure the highlight fabrics travel through all the blocks.

- **For 12–20 crazy quilt blocks**

  Choose about 30 fabrics. This way you can have several selections of a chosen color—such as 5 blacks, 5 greens, 5 purples, 5 rusts, 5 golds, and 5 blues. The highlight fabrics can travel throughout the quilt but not appear in every block.

CHOOSING SUPPLIES

After deciding on the size and colors of the crazy quilt project, pull all the supplies you think you will need. Always pull the fabrics and foundation fabric first, because after the blocks are started you cannot change your mind.

After the fabrics are pulled, I cut working pieces (12″ × 12″ squares are good) and then set the larger pieces of fabric aside. I cut all the foundation pieces at the same time.

Next, I pull the laces, trims, and ribbons. If the laces and medallions are too light for the project, I dye them using Colorhue Instant-Set Silk Dyes. These are instant-take dyes and are very easy to use. Be sure to have a good variety of choices and enough of the chosen pieces to use throughout the project.

Photos by Judith Baker Montano

I choose the embroidery threads and silk ribbons in advance and decide which of these will act as highlights. Beads, doodads, and buttons are pulled and kept on a separate tray. I use three or four trays to keep my supplies separated and ready.

THE MONTANO CENTERPIECE METHOD

I came up with this machine piecing method in the 80s because how-to books on crazy quilting did not exist. The traditional method of piecing with hand appliqué and embroidery was too slow for me. I wanted a faster piecing process so that I could get to the embroidery and the embellishments!

For a crazy quilt, large or small, you must work on a square or rectangular foundation (muslin). I recommend working on a 12″ × 12″ square or smaller because the piecing is easier to handle.

If you are right-handed, be sure to work in a clockwise motion to fill in all the angles. If you are left-handed, work counterclockwise.

My cardinal rule:

In traditional crazy quilting I have one cardinal rule: Never put pattern against pattern! Always "bounce" patterns against solids and textured solids. If you use busy patterns against busy patterns, the embroidery stitches will not show, and that is the highlight of a crazy quilt. I work hard to arrange the patterned fabrics against solid fabrics and to bounce the cool and warm colors off each other.

Note the pleasing mix of solids, patterns, and textures. There is a good mix of fabric types, with a balance of cool and warm colors. The embellishments and stitches create a complementary mix.

Photo by Judith Baker Montano

1. Choose a solid fabric and cut a 5-sided piece. This will act as the centerpiece. Place the 5-sided centerpiece on the muslin, and set it off-center. Make sure that none of the sides are parallel to the outside edges. It must be off-center in all ways.

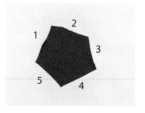

3. It is not necessary to use ¼″ seams. Sometimes a wider or narrower seam will be better. Trim the seam if it is wider than ¼″. Flip over the rectangle and steam press.

2. Cut a wide rectangle (2½″–3″) that is long enough to overlap each end of Angle 1. Make sure it is a print that complements the solid center. Place the rectangle right sides together along the edge of the centerpiece. Sew from end to end of Angle 1.

4. Place the second rectangle along Angle 2, covering the previous rectangle. From now on there will always be a previous piece to cover. Sew from the end of the previous piece to the end of Angle 2 of the solid centerpiece. Trim along the new seamline. Flip over the rectangle to the right side and steam press.

5. I use *pieced rectangles and curves* in Round 1 to make my crazy quilting look more collaged. For Angle 3, I use a curved angle. To do this, cut a wider rectangle with a curve on one side. Be sure it is long enough to cover the angle and the previous piece. Clip the curved edges, use a glue stick to secure them to the back of the piece, and then steam press.

6. Place the curved rectangle down on Angle 3 and mark with a white pencil. Trim the seam to ¼″ and glue the curved rectangle into place, using a glue stick. It is not sewn down; it will be held in place by the next piece of fabric.

7. Sew the next rectangle along Angle 4. Notice that this will hold the curved rectangle in place until it can be appliquéd down.

Note: I make *Montano mitered rectangles* to give the illusion of more angles and to use more of my chosen fabrics. This avoids using long strips of fabrics. You can make the angle very steep or shallow, and you can decide which way the angle will lie.

8. Cut 2 rectangle pieces the same width. Place them right side up, as they will be when sewn together. Place them beside the next angle on the centerpiece to decide the direction of the mitered angle. Make sure it does not line up with any previous angles, as this creates a stripy look! Make sure patterns are not next to each other.

9. Feel the fabric of the 2 rectangles and cut the angle on the heavier fabric. The cut angle will become a guideline. Place the fabrics, right side up, exactly as they will be when sewn together into a rectangle.

10. Fold the lighter-weight piece along the cut angle and press with your fingers. This will create a crease in the lighter-weight fabric.

Photos by Judith Baker Montano

11. Hold together the 2 pieces, turn them to the back, and slip your thumb under the flap of the lighter-weight fabric. Make sure that the crease and the cut angle of the heavier fabric are lined up. Sew along the angled cut line of the heavier fabric.

12. Cut away the flap of the lighter fabric and press the seam open. Don't worry if the long edges are not exactly even, as you can trim them down. This method is the answer to filling in long sides and gives a more mosaic look to your work.

13. Place this mitered rectangle along Angle 5, right sides together, covering the previous rectangle and the first rectangle piece. Place the mitered rectangle so equal amounts of the 2 fabrics will show. Stitch the piece in place. Trim any fabrics that hang beyond the foundation edges.

14. Cut seamline to seamline to create angles for Round 2. Always create as many angles as possible; in this case, 6 angles have been created. Choose the beginning angle of Round 2; in this case, it is in the lower left corner. Sew Angle 1 of Round 2 in place.

Note: I use *pie wedges* (fan shapes) to fill in long lines. They also allow for several fabrics to be used along 1 line.

15. Cover Angle 2; in this case, it is covered with a curved rectangle. Angle 3 is now a very long line. Use pie wedges or fan shapes to cover long lines. This enables you to use many different fabrics and adds interest to the work. Draw a line along the long angle. Choose a pivot point for the pie wedges. For guidance, draw the lines of the pie wedges using a water-erasable pen.

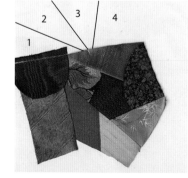

16. Work with rectangle shapes and always bounce cool colors against warm colors and patterns against solids. Always start at the top of the wedge and sew down, toward the pivot point.

17. With right sides together, always sew beyond the previous point by 1 stitch. Cut closely along the seam. Steam press each wedge as you go.

18. The last rectangle (wedge) is folded under as an appliqué seam. Trim out the excess from behind and use a glue stick to secure in place.

19. Angle 4 of Round 2 has been covered by a mitered rectangle (see Steps 8–12, page 123). Be aware that Rounds 2 and 3 will require all pieced curves (see Steps 5 and 6, page 123), mitered rectangles, and pie wedges for a mosaic look.

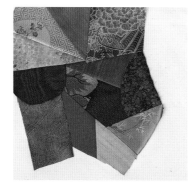

20. Angle 5 of Round 2 is covered by a pieced rectangle with undulating curves. Use a mix of convex and concave curves for added interest. Use both on the same rectangle for undulating curves.

21. The mitered rectangle on Angle 6 of Round 2 completes this round. Now it is time to cut the final angles for Round 3.

22. There are only 4 angles for Round 3. Check to see where you can use the dominant fabrics.

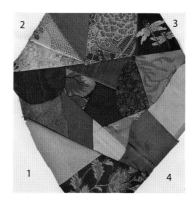

Photos by Judith Baker Montano

23. Here is the finished square. A pieced concave rectangle has been added to the lower left corner. This pulls the color throughout the block.

An undulating piece in the lower right features an embroidered flower. Steam press the front and back of the block. Trim the block to the desired size.

24. The next process is to place the ribbons, lace, and trims. These large embellishments are placed down before the embroidery. This way they do not

cover any embroidered seams. Arrange the trims, lace, and ribbons so that raw edges will be caught in a seam. Do not place them along a seam—save the seamlines for embroidery. Note how the lace slips under the black curved piece (left side).

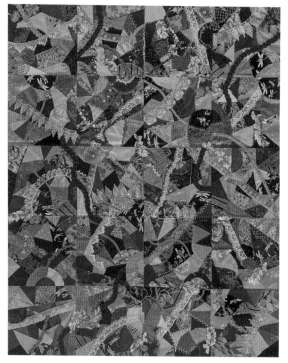

Twenty-block crazy quilt top

Photos by Judith Baker Montano

Piecing Together Blocks

When you are planning to piece together blocks, make sure that the fabrics along the joining seams complement each other. After two blocks are pieced, I pin them to a foam core board for reference. It is now very important that all the following blocks complement each other. I add the blocks as they are pieced to see how the colors and shapes are flowing. Sometimes I let the same fabric (on two different blocks) butt together on the joining seam. This gives the illusion of being one piece and blurs the joining seams.

Note: Do not piece together blocks until after the ribbons, lace, and trims are added.

PREPARING FOR EMBROIDERY

Note: *After a block has been pieced, steam pressed, and trimmed to size, there will be several loose seams (curves, pie wedges, and so on) that will require tacking. Do not do this yet! Wait until the large embellishments are in place. Sometimes these loose seams are perfect for hiding the raw edges of meandering embellishments.*

Placing Lace, Ribbons, and Trims

Begin by deciding just how much embellishment you want to use. The mood or feel of the project often dictates the number of embellishments used. Some projects call out for lots of laces, ribbons, and trims while others will need only a few metallic trims and lots of embroidery. My rule of thumb is never to allow the embellishments to take over the project. Leave room for fabrics to show through, and leave the seamlines clear for embroidery stitches.

After the crazy quilt blocks are pieced and pinned on the design wall, I then decide on the number and types of embellishments. I choose a set number of trims, laces, and ribbons to add to each block before I join together the blocks.

Check the pulled embellishment materials to make sure there will be enough of each to travel throughout the quilt. Sometimes the unifying factor is color, such as several types of lace all dyed one color. Sometimes it will be a specific trim or ribbon.

The trims, ribbons, and laces are placed down in several stages— before the blocks are joined together and after. Decide on the number of pieces to use on each block and glue these into place, using a glue stick.

Victorian Actresses, by Judith Baker Montano, 48″ × 48″

This is a heavily embroidered and embellished crazy quilt featuring original Victorian cigarette silks.

Chicken Bumble Pincushion

BY JUDITH BAKER MONTANO

Photo by Judith Baker Montano

FINISHED PINCUSHION: 4″ × 4½″

A bumble was originally a Victorian baby toy. I was gifted with a crazy quilted bumble in Australia and fell in love with it. Later I saw a rooster bumble made with quilted squares—and then made one for my friend Phyl Drew. They are fun to make and wonderful pincushion gifts. If you wish to make a traditional bumble, simply leave off the beak, wattle, and tail feathers.

MATERIALS AND SUPPLIES

FOUNDATIONS: 2 squares 5″ × 5″ of muslin

FANCY FABRICS (SOLIDS, PRINTS, AND TEXTURES): 8 small pieces

TAIL:

1 square 4½″ × 4½″ of fancy fabric

1 square 3½″ × 3½″ of fancy fabric

WATTLE AND COMB: 1 square 4″ × 4″ of red fabric

BEAK: 1 square 2″ × 2″ of gold fabric

EMBROIDERY THREADS (various colors and styles)

SILK RIBBONS (various colors and styles)

NEEDLES: embroidery, chenille, and tapestry

EMBELLISHMENTS: lace, ribbons, and trims

BEADS, NYMO BEADING THREAD, AND #10 SHARPS NEEDLE

TEMPLATE PLASTIC: 1 square 8″ × 8″

POLYESTER FIBERFILL

EYES: 2 black beads

Crazy Quilting and Embellishment

1. Trace the chicken bumble pattern (page 130) onto template plastic and cut out along the cutting line. Trace the comb and wattle patterns onto template plastic and cut out.

2. Fill in the 2 muslin squares with crazy quilting or embroidery stitches. Keep the pieces small.

3. Place the window template on the crazy quilt squares and move it around until you find a pleasing design. Mark the outline with the water-erasable pen. Cut out on the cutting line.

4. Embellish and embroider the crazy quilt pieces. Add beads, buttons, and doodads. Set aside.

Pincushion Assembly

1. Fold the 4½″ × 4½″ tail square into a prairie point and press.

2. Fold the 3½″ × 3½″ tail square into a prairie point and press. Pin this prairie point on top of the prairie point from Step 1, as shown.

3. Mark and cut 2 red wattles and 2 red combs. Sew on the sewing line, turn right side out, and press. Add additional embroidery to the wattle and comb as desired. Pin in place on a crazy quilt square.

4. Fold the gold 2″ × 2″ square into a prairie point; then fold

again. Pin in place on the beak area, folded side up.

Pin the three pieces (wattle, comb, and beak) in the designated areas.

5. Place the crazy quilt squares right sides together. Sew on the sides designated 1, 2, and 3.

6. Turn right side out. Match up the seamlines of side 1 and side 3. Press down to form a center fold on each side.

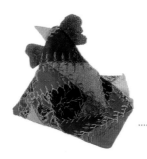

7. Pin and sew the tail pieces on top of the side 1 seam. Trim the excess tail fabric.

8. Turn wrong side out and sew 1″ in at the center fold on each side. Turn right side out and stuff the bumble with polyester batting. Hand stitch the opening closed.

9. Sew the eyes in place. Sew a bead on and through to the other side. Pull it in a bit to create an indentation.

Photos by Judith Baker Montano

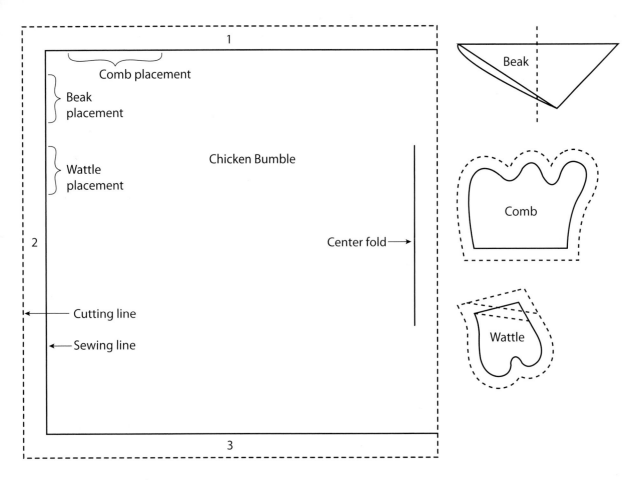

1

Comb placement

Beak placement

Wattle placement

Chicken Bumble

2

Center fold →

Cutting line

Sewing line

3

Beak

Comb

Wattle

English Paper Piecing

BY SUE DALEY

HELPFUL TOOLS

Rotating Cutting Board

I used to call this a luxury item, but now I call it a necessity. I use the Patchwork with Busyfingers boards, which allow me to turn the board as I rotary cut around each side of a template. The 10˝ board is great for traveling or cutting on your lap. The 16˝ board is wonderful for using at home in your studio. I also use these boards while glue-basting the fabric to the paper shapes.

Busyfingers rotating cutting board

Sandpaper Board

Perfect for tracing appliqué templates onto fabric, a sandpaper board will grip the fabric and keep it from moving while you trace. Place the fabric right side up on the sandpaper side of the board. Place the template on the fabric and trace around it.

Template Paper or Freezer Paper

This is used for making appliqué templates. My preference is template paper, a heavy-duty tracing or drafting paper, because it is reusable.

Thread

I use cotton thread with cotton fabric in most cases. The exception is when I am doing English paper piecing and needle-turn appliqué. Then my thread of choice is Superior Bottom Line thread. I use this in preference to cotton for English paper piecing because cotton thread shreds as it is continually pulled across the top of the cards during piecing. Superior Bottom Line is a strong, fine polyester thread that blends well and doesn't shred.

Superior Bottom Line thread

Needles

I recommend a milliner's or straw needle in size 11, or size 10 if you prefer a slightly larger eye. The finer the needle, the finer your work will be. My preference is the Patchwork with Busyfingers size 11 needles.

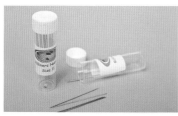

Busyfingers milliner's/straw needles

Paper Shapes

You can cut the shapes out of heavy paper, but if you want to save time you can use the Patchwork with Busyfingers precut paper pieces, which come in a variety of sizes and shapes. Packs include approximately 50 precut papers and an acrylic template for rotary cutting each fabric shape with the seam allowance. For large projects, when you need more than 50 precut papers, bulk packs are available.

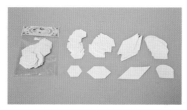

Busyfingers precut paper pieces

Acrylic Templates

I recommend the Patchwork with Busyfingers templates, which include the seam allowances. You can rotary cut around these through many layers of fabric on your rotating cutting mat.

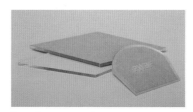

Busyfingers acrylic templates

Glue

Appliqué glue   My glue of choice is Patchwork with Busyfingers Appliqué Glue. This glue is used instead of pins to attach appliqué shapes to the background fabric while you sew. It should be used sparingly, just a few small spots here and there.

Busyfingers Appliqué Glue

English paper-piecing glue
The Sewline Fabric Glue Pen is ideal for basting the fabric to the paper shapes. Glue-basting saves so much time over thread-basting!

Sewline Fabric Glue Pen and refill

Marking Pencils

There are many marking pencils on the market. The Sewline Trio pencil has ceramic leads, and with one twist of the pencil you can change the color of the lead.

Sewline Trio pencil

Scissors

Small embroidery scissors are ideal for snipping threads and cutting out small fabric shapes.

General sewing scissors are ideal for cutting larger pieces of fabric.

Paper scissors are used for cutting only paper, such as template paper or freezer paper.

Batting/Wadding

For machine quilting, I recommend cotton or a poly/wool blend.

For hand quilting, I recommend a low-loft polydown.

ENGLISH PAPER-PIECING TECHNIQUES

These instructions apply to all shapes when paper piecing.

1. Cut the fabric ¼″ larger than the paper shape, all the way around. If you are using an acrylic Patchwork with Busy-fingers template, fold the fabric into layers, place the template on top of the fabric, and rotary cut around the shape.

2. Place each fabric shape wrong side up and place the paper shape on top, being careful to centre the paper shape.

3. Fold the seam allowances to the back of each paper shape and baste them in place.

NOTE *Some of the shapes, such as the hexagon, have corners that will fold in neatly. Shapes with smaller points, like the diamond, will have tails hanging out behind the point. Leave the tails hanging out, making sure that the fabric is basted tightly around the paper shape.*

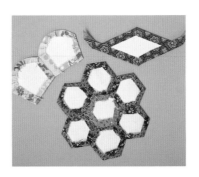

Glue-Basting Method

Using the Sewline Fabric Glue Pen to baste the seam allowances will cut your basting time by about 75%.

1. Run the glue stick along one side of the paper shape, being careful not to get any glue on the fabric. (This would cause a buildup, making it difficult to stitch through.)

tip Don't use too much glue. In warm weather, the glue in the pen can become soft, making it easy to use too much. I suggest putting the pen in the refrigerator for a few minutes before using it.

2. Fold the fabric over and hold it for a moment. Continue around the shape until all sides are folded over.

3. When you are ready to remove the paper, just peel the fabric away. It's even easier than taking out thread-basting because you don't have the hassle of unpicking all the basting thread.

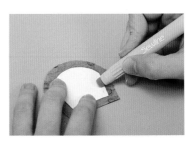

Glue application

Assembling the Pieces

1. Place the right sides of 2 pieces together and whipstitch the seam from corner to corner. Start with a knot in the thread. Sew 2 or 3 stitches on top of each other to start. Taking small bites of fabric, sew with a whipstitch, approximately 16 stitches to the inch. Finish by making 2 stitches in the corner and overstitching 2 stitches back.

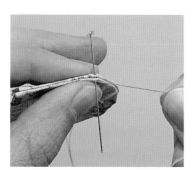

Beginning of the whipstitch

Whipstitch, 16 stitches to the inch

2. In most designs, you can sew pieces together in any order.

3. Open the pair. With a dry iron, give the set a press on the right side.

tip Inset Seams

Inset seams are easy with English paper piecing because you stitch only from corner to corner on each piece.

With right sides together, sew a seam with a whipstitch. When you get to the corner, just refold the pieces and realign the next edges you need to sew. English paper piecing helps you achieve perfect corners.

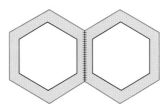

Hexagon paper-piecing assembly

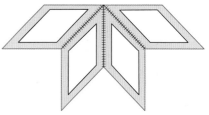

Eight-pointed star paper-piecing assembly

4. If you are making blocks that will be pieced to other blocks, you can remove the paper piece from each block as soon as it is surrounded and stabilized by other blocks. Press your work on the right side before removing the papers. The papers can then be reused a number of times.

Foundation Piecing

BY JANE HALL AND DIXIE HAYWOOD

Piecing on a foundation has become a boon to quiltmakers of all levels of expertise. A foundation is any material that you stitch *on* or *with* to provide stability and precision. This old-made-new technique uses an extra element in the piecing process and is an easily mastered approach to quiltmaking.

FOUNDATION TYPES

A *permanent foundation* of fabric or interfacing remains in the piece. A *temporary foundation*, made of various types of papers or removable interfacing, is torn out when the piecing is complete.

The choice of foundation is often influenced by the type of quilt—bed, wall, or wearable; the kind of quilting or embellishment planned; and the availability of material. Lightweight foundations are often the best choice. Many papers and interfacings are translucent, which is also desirable.

FOUNDATION MATERIALS

Permanent

Fabric   Fabric can act as interfacing for clothing and gives stability to machine quilting. It adds bulk when hand quilting. Match the weight of the foundation fabric to the project. Fabric should be preshrunk.

Interfacing   Has the same qualities as fabric. Do *not* use bias interfacing.

Flannel   This can be used as a combination foundation and filler. Flannel should be preshrunk.

Batting or fleece   This material can be used to piece and quilt in one step. Be sure to use it with fabric backing to avoid distortion.

Temporary

Tracing paper   This paper is translucent, easy to mark, and easy to remove. However, it may tear prematurely.

Tear-away interfacing   Like tracing paper, this is a translucent material. It is less likely to tear prematurely. It can also act as a permanent foundation.

Vellum tracing paper   Although this is more expensive than interfacing or tracing paper, it is less likely to tear prematurely.

Examining room table paper   Similar to tracing paper, this inexpensive paper is especially useful when a long foundation is needed.

Freezer paper   Freezer paper is good for difficult-to-control fabric or when a long foundation is needed. However, it is more difficult to remove when pressed repeatedly, and it is not as pliable as some materials. Use the shiny side against fabric.

Adhesive paper   This paper, which adheres well, is good for single foundations sewn by hand or machine. *Do not iron*, as it melts with heat.

Preprinted foundations   Many patterns are available on preprinted foundations in pads or sheets.

Typing or photocopy paper   This is not the best option, as it is not translucent and it may tear prematurely. You also must use very small machine stitches to avoid distortion when it is removed.

MARKING THE FOUNDATION

Most of the techniques require you to mark the pattern on the foundation. Your choice of marking techniques may depend on the foundation material you're using or what you have available. Either way, there is a wide variety from which to choose.

Before you begin, you will need to decide the piecing order for sewing the patches and then mark that information on the foundation. Some blocks have options for the first piece. Other patterns have only one possible starting place. You also must decide whether the foundation will be the finished size of the block or will include a ¼″ seam allowance on all sides. Including the seam allowance in the foundation can provide more stability, but doing so requires picking out the small bits of foundation from the seam allowance.

Marking Tools and Techniques

Tracing   When tracing, use a thin-lead pencil and a transparent ruler for accuracy. Tracing is tedious for multiples but useful for a quick sample block. Avoid pens, which may transfer to fabric when pressed.

Computer printing or digital copy based on a scanned image This produces very accurate images. Be sure to use the thinnest paper your printer will handle.

Hot iron transfer This technique is good for marking multiple copies on fabric. Use a transfer pencil to make a hot iron transfer. Sharpen the pencil often to keep a consistent point when drawing the transfer.

Stamps and stencils Many patterns of stamps and stencils are available. Most are small and traditional. Many office supply companies can make a custom stamp.

Tracing wheel With the use of dressmaker's carbon paper, multiple copies can be made using a dressmaker's tracing wheel on paper or fabric.

Photocopy Avoid photocopying if possible. Even the best machine can distort the image, usually in only one direction, making a slightly rectangular block. If you must photocopy, always use the original. Never copy a copy.

Needle punch This is our favorite method for making accurate multiple foundations on paper. The process results

in a neat stack of identical patterns, firmly held together by the punching of the sewing machine. All kinds of paper can be needle punched; tracing paper is especially suitable. However, this technique does not work well for fabric or interfacing, because the holes are not visible.

1. Unthread your sewing machine, both top and bobbin.

2. Pin a pattern onto a stack of up to 12 sheets of lightweight paper. Staple or use a few pins to anchor the stack together.

3. Beginning in the middle of the pattern, stitch on all the lines in one plane. Stitch on the remaining lines in that plane, then all the remaining lines in the block, including the outside lines.

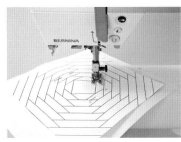
Needle punching a stack of paper

4. Check on the back of the stack of patterns to make sure you have sewn on all lines.

5. If you want the foundations to be the finished size, trim the excess paper on the outside block

lines, leaving a small tab on one corner to make it easy to separate the pages.

A tab to help separate the papers

tip If you are needle punching freezer paper, the waxy side will slip easily against the feed dogs. To fool the feed dogs, position a piece of fabric under the stack of paper. The needle punching will then be quick and easy.

THE TECHNIQUES

There are three basic techniques using foundations, plus several variations within these techniques. In these examples, the foundation is the finished size.

Top *Pressed Piecing*

Top pressed piecing is the oldest technique, used in the U.S. in the latter half of the nineteenth century for Log Cabin patterns. It was also used for the Pineapple, a Log Cabin variation, and later for crazy piecing and string designs. The latter two create appealing designs by themselves and add texture to blocks, backgrounds, and borders.

DIAGONAL-STRING PIECED BLOCK

1. Pin the first fabric piece to the foundation, right side up. Pin the second piece facedown on the first, matching cut edges.

Pin the first pieces to the foundation.

2. Stitch on the fabric through all layers, using a ¼″ seam allowance.

Stitching the second piece to the first

3. Open the second piece and press against the foundation. Pin in place. Repeat Steps 2 and 3 until the foundation is covered with fabric.

Second piece opened and pinned to the foundation.

4. Press the block flat and trim the excess seam allowance to ¼″.

Trimming the finished block

Back of finished block

Finished block

If you use irregularly shaped pieces of fabric and strips with this technique, it becomes crazy piecing, which provides even more texture.

Crazy-pieced block

Paper Piecing

BY ALEX ANDERSON

Using unusual, challenging fabrics—such as flannel, silk, and rayon—is easily manageable with foundation paper piecing. The paper keeps the fabric stable while you are stitching pieces together. Blocks with exposed bias edges and tiny points are made easy using paper piecing. You can approach difficult patterns with the confidence that they will come out perfectly.

I find it very helpful to precut fabric shapes larger than necessary. If you are cutting strips, cut each strip at least ½″ wider and longer than the section you will cover on the pattern. If you are using half-square triangle shapes, cut the square at least 1″ larger than the section you will cover on the pattern, then cut diagonally from corner to corner. For quarter-square triangles, cut the square at least 1½″ larger, then cut diagonally from corner to corner, twice. In each of the projects in this book I will give you precutting sizes.

After each seam is sewn, you will trim the fabric shape leaving a ¼″ seam allowance.

PATTERNS

Paper-piecing patterns are meant to be photocopied. Sometimes distortion can occur when photocopying, so be sure to test the accuracy of a sample photocopy by measuring it against the original before making all the necessary photocopies.

Note that the sewing order is indicated by numbers. Simply sew each piece in numerical order, trim, and press. Easy as that!

SEWING NOTES

In general, you will set your machine stitch length to 18–20 stitches per inch. The stitches should be tight enough to perforate the paper for easy paper removal, but not so tight that seam ripping becomes an impossible task. Make adjustments as you see necessary. Use an 80/12 or 90/14 universal or sharp needle. They are a little heavier, which helps penetrate both the fabric and paper and makes paper removal easier.

When sewing, stitch two or three stitches beyond the drawn line. This allows the next line of stitches to lock the previous line of stitches in place.

When sewing the blocks together into rows, remove the paper in the seam allowances before sewing the rows together. This allows you to press the seams in opposite directions before sewing the rows together.

Do not remove the remaining paper until the project instructions tell you to do so. To tear out the paper, gently run your seam ripper's long pointed tip along the seamline. It helps to weaken the paper and makes for easier removal. You can also weaken the paper by machine stitching on the lines without thread before you start paper piecing. This adds more holes in the paper and makes the paper tear more easily.

If you have to remove and resew a seam, cut every third or fourth stitch on one side, then gently lift the thread off of the other side. If there are so many holes in the paper that it falls apart, use removable clear tape sparingly to hold the paper in place until you finish paper piecing. Be careful not to iron over it, or use Sewer's Fix-it Tape, which can be ironed over.

PRESSING

I prefer ironing to finger-pressing because I've seen quilters get too aggressive and stretch fabric out of shape.

Do not use steam in your iron! The water in the steam can distort and weaken the paper.

It is very important to press properly and thoroughly when paper piecing. If you are careless, tucks will be permanently pressed into the block. Many people like to "set the seams" first by simply pressing on the sewn line. This helps to lock the stitches into place. After setting the seam, flip the fabric over so that you see the right side of the fabric; press again. Make sure to avoid any tucks. A mini iron is wonderful. Try to avoid pressing directly on the printed side of the paper. It can smudge and dirty your iron plate. I use a thin tea towel to cover the pressing surface so the ink doesn't stain my ironing board.

Square-in-a-Square

BY ALEX ANDERSON

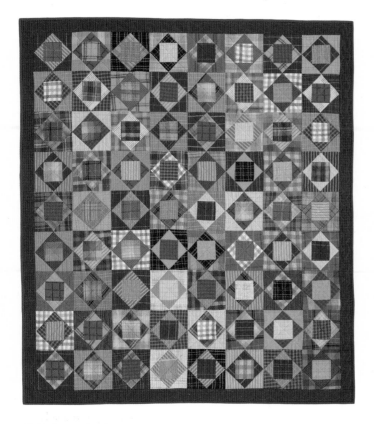

FINISHED BLOCK: 6″ × 6″

FINISHED QUILT: 52½″ × 58½″

Paper pieced by Alex Anderson,
machine quilted by Paula Reid

MATERIALS

The following instructions give the total amount of yardage needed to complete your quilt and are based on a 42″ fabric width.

BLOCKS: 2 yards of light-colored flannels

BLOCKS: 2 yards of dark-colored flannels

BORDER: ½ yard

BACKING: 3⅓ yards

BATTING: 56″ × 62″

BINDING: ½ yard

Square-in-a-Square Block

CUTTING

You will need 72 blocks. Make 36 A blocks that begin with a dark center and 36 B blocks that begin with a light center.

ROUGH CUT (FOR EACH A BLOCK)

DARK CENTER SQUARE 1:
Cut 1 square 3½″ × 3½″.

LIGHT TRIANGLES 2 AND 3:
Cut 2 squares 3½″ × 3½″; subcut in half diagonally.

DARK TRIANGLES 4 AND 5:
Cut 2 squares 4½″ × 4½″; subcut in half diagonally.

ROUGH CUT (FOR EACH B BLOCK)

LIGHT CENTER SQUARE 1:
Cut 1 square 3½″ × 3½″.

DARK TRIANGLES 2 AND 3:
Cut 2 squares 3½″ × 3½″; subcut in half diagonally.

LIGHT TRIANGLES 4 AND 5:
Cut 2 squares 4½″ × 4½″; subcut in half diagonally.

PIECING

1. Make 72 copies of the paper pattern (page 141) and cut out the paper pattern just outside the dashed line.

2. Place the paper pattern printed side down.

3. Position the center square (#1), right side up, on the unprinted side of the paper pattern. For a thicker paper, hold it up to the light to help position the center square.

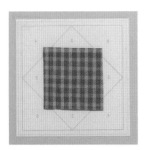

Position center square.

4. Place 2 light triangles (#2) on top of the center square, with right sides together, matching the raw edges. Pin.

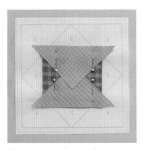

Place triangles and pin.

5. Turn the paper pattern over and stitch on both lines between #1 and #2.

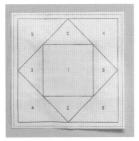

Stitch.

6. Press open.

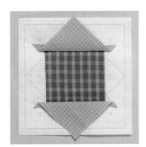

Press.

7. Place 2 more light triangles (#3) on opposite sides of the center square, with right sides together, matching the raw edges. Pin.

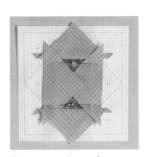

Place triangles and pin.

8. Turn the paper pattern over and stitch on both lines between #1 and #3.

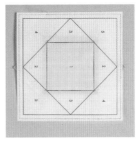

Stitch.

9. Press open.

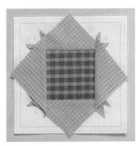

Press.

10. Fold the paper on one of the lines between #2/#3 and #4.

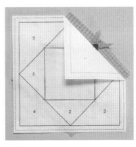

Fold.

11. Trim the seam allowance to ¼˝.

8. Turn the paper pattern over and stitch on both lines between #1 and #3.

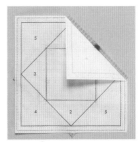

Trim.

12. Repeat Steps 10 and 11 for the 3 remaining edges.

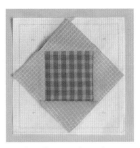

Fold and trim the other 3 edges.

13. Place 2 dark triangles (#4) on opposite sides of the new square on the lines between #2/#3 and #4, with right sides together, matching the raw edge with the just-trimmed edge. Pin.

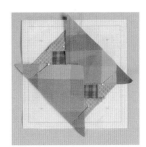

Place triangles and pin.

14. Turn the paper pattern over and stitch along the line between #2/#3 and #4.

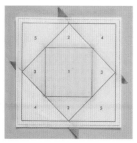

Stitch.

15. Press open.

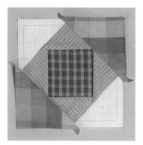

Press.

16. Place 2 more dark triangles (#5) on opposite sides of the square on the lines between #2/#3 and #5, with right sides together, matching the raw edge with the edge that was previously trimmed. Pin.

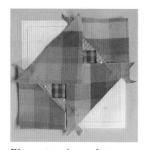

Place triangles and pin.

17. Stitch on the line.

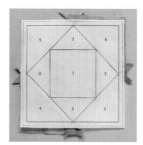

Stitch.

18. Press open.

Press.

19. Place the block with the paper on top and trim on the dashed line.

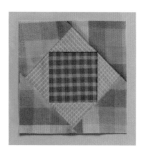

Completed block

20. Repeat these steps to make a total of 36 A blocks and 36 B blocks.

QUILT TOP CONSTRUCTION

Press, following the arrows in the diagram (below).

1. Arrange your blocks in a straight set, alternating the A and B blocks as shown. Make sure that every block is an alternate value colored block.

2. Sew the blocks into rows. Press. Sew the rows together. Press.

Border

1. Cut 3 strips 2½″ × fabric width. Piece into 1 long strip and trim into 2 strips 2½″ × 54½″. Sew onto the sides. Press.

2. Repeat Step 1, this time cutting 2 strips 2½″ × 52½″. Sew onto the top and bottom. Press.

3. Remove the paper.

FINISHING

For details on sandwiching and quilting, refer to Chapter 5: Quilting by Hand and Machine (page 86). For details on binding your project, refer to Binding Your Quilt (page 114).

Layer, baste, quilt, and bind the quilt as desired.

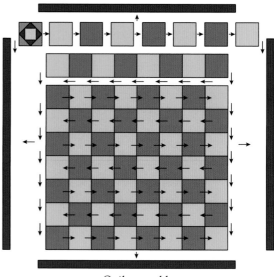

Quilt assembly

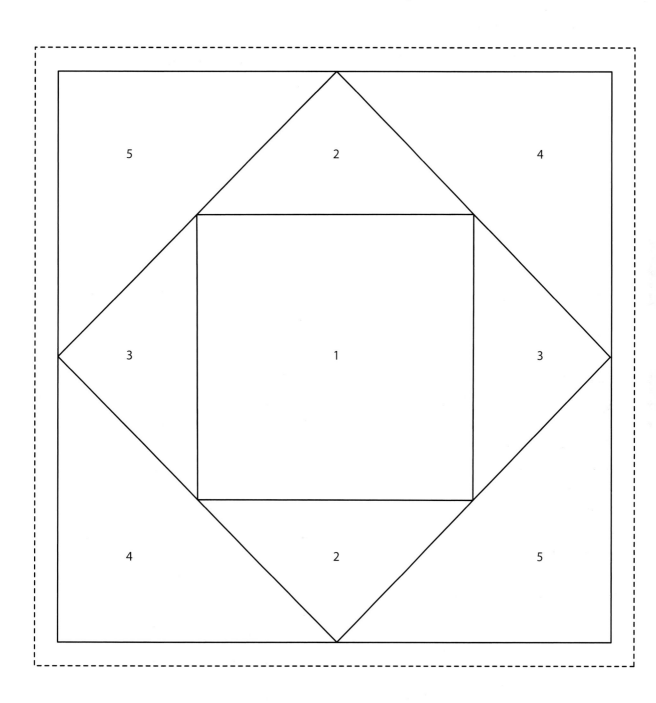

Quilt-As-You-Go

BY JERA BRANDVIG

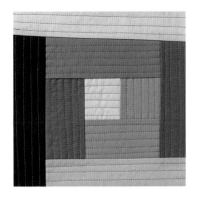

My style of quilting-as-you-go is similar to foundation/paper piecing, except the fabric is pieced directly onto small batting blocks instead of paper. This technique is a style of improvisational quilting, but you can use it to make quilts as abstract or structured as you want.

QUILT-AS-YOU-GO LOG CABIN BLOCK

Learn to make a traditional Log Cabin–style block using the quilt-as-you-go technique. You will quilt straight lines onto each patch, building a beautiful quilting pattern that will look like it took hours to create!

MATERIALS

BATTING: 1 square 1˝ bigger than block's trim size

FABRIC: Strips 2½˝ × width of fabric

Construction

Use a ¼˝ seam allowance for piecing and quilt assembly unless specified otherwise.

1. Use fabric scissors to cut a square from the end of a fabric strip. It is okay if it is not an exact square.

2. Place the fabric square in the center of the batting square. Quilt  a design onto the square, using straight lines.

3. From a different strip, cut a square approximately the same size 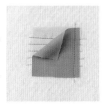 as the square you just quilted.

Place the second square on top of the first, right sides together, aligning an edge that is perpendicular to the quilting lines on the first square. Sew along that edge.

4. Press the seam open, doing your best to avoid ironing the batting. Quilt the second square directly onto the batting using straight lines parallel to the new seam.

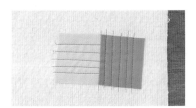

By quilting each piece individually, you will create a beautiful and intricate labyrinth of quilting.

tips

• When quilting, start and end the stitching line off the fabric and on the batting. There is no need to backstitch. Don't put an important part of the quilting design in the outer ¼˝ of the fabric, though, because this section will become the seam allowance.

• Use a stitch length of 3.5 on a scale of 0–5. This length is not small enough to create bunching, but also not long enough to be a basting stitch.

- If the fabric starts to bunch or pucker, try using an even-feed walking foot.

- Get into the habit of trimming the trailing threads. If your sewing machine has an automatic thread cutter that quickly snips the thread with a push of the button, then you are in luck! You'll soon find that button to be your new best friend.

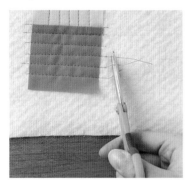

5. From a third strip, cut a length to match the 2 squares that you just quilted. Place the third strip on top of the first 2, right sides facing together. Align an edge along the length of the first 2 pieces and sew.

6. Press open. Quilt straight lines parallel to the new seam.

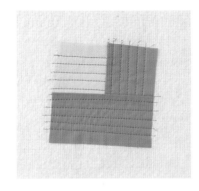

7. From a fourth strip, cut a length to match the width of the first and third pieces. Use the same process to attach and quilt it, stitching the quilted lines parallel to the new seam.

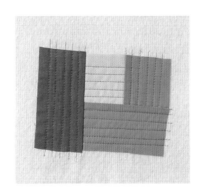

8. Repeat with a fifth strip.

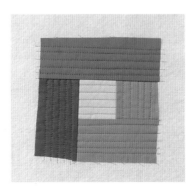

9. Continue to add strips and quilt each with lines parallel to the new seams. Build on the central patchwork until you cover the batting with pieced and quilted strips. In this example, I added fabric in a clockwise direction. You will have extra fabric around the edge of the batting. You can trim and square up the block later.

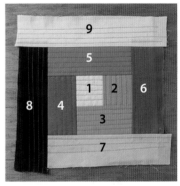

Front of block, covered with pieced, quilted strips

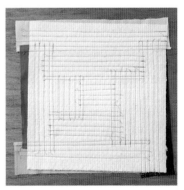

Back of block

FOUR SIMPLE QUILT-AS-YOU-GO GUIDELINES

BY JERA BRANDVIG

1. When you piece fabric onto the batting, the pieces have to build upon the initial patchwork. Do not quilt one piece to the batting and then add another strip off in a random corner. Add to the initial fabric piece so that it grows bigger until patchwork eventually covers the entire batting square.

2. When you add a strip, cut it the same length as the edge where it will be attached. If you add a shorter or longer strip, you will create an angle in the patchwork that you cannot piece over with a single ¼″ seam allowance.

3. Start and end the stitching line on the batting when possible. When you get to the outer edge of the batting, start and end the stitches on the excess fabric hanging off the edge of the batting. There is no need to backstitch.

4. If you plan to quilt each piece individually, the general rule of thumb is to make the quilting lines run parallel to the new seam.

SQUARING UP THE BLOCKS

After you have completely covered the batting, the block is ready to be trimmed to a perfect square ½″ larger than the finished size of the block. This is called *squaring up the block.*

NOTE: *I highly recommend using a rotating cutting mat because you can efficiently trim all four sides of a block without having to pick up and reposition the block.* It will be easier to trim the blocks if you have a square ruler the same size as the trimmed block. In this book, the trimmed block sizes are usually 9½″ or 12½″ square.

An alternative to buying square rulers is to cut a square of template plastic to match the trim size of the block. To use the template as a guide, align a cutting ruler along the edge of the template and trim with a rotary cutter.

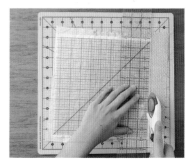

To use a plastic template, align a ruler with the edge of the template and cut.

Improvisational Square-Up Technique

Use this method if you are *not* trying to cut the front of the block a specific way. This method works well for blocks that have an improvisational or abstract look.

1. Place the block on the cutting mat with the batting side facing you.

2. Position the square ruler or template on the block so that it is within the batting and as centered as possible.

3. Use a rotary cutter to trim the excess fabric on all 4 sides.

With the batting facing you, position the ruler within the batting and trim all 4 sides.

Squared-up block

Precise Square-Up Technique

Use this technique when you want the front of the block trimmed a specific way. In this method, you will finish squaring up the block with the front of the block facing you.

1. Place the block on the cutting mat with the batting side facing you. Align a ruler with the edge of the batting and trim the excess fabric from all 4 sides.

With the batting facing you, trim the excess fabric outside the batting.

2. Turn the block over so the front faces up. Position the square ruler or template to your specific needs.

3. Use a rotary cutter to trim excess fabric on all 4 sides.

Turn the block front side up. Position the ruler and trim all 4 sides.

Squared-up block

QUILTING TECHNIQUES

Quilting each piece onto the batting individually is just one option for how to quilt a block. Here are some other ideas.

No Quilting

This block was pieced directly onto the batting, and that was it. The result is similar to stitch-in-the-ditch quilting. To add more quilting, you could always quilt an allover design on the entire block after it is pieced.

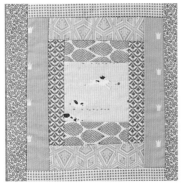

Front of block with no quilting

Back of block with no quilting

Overlap Quilting

Piece two or three strips of fabric onto the batting and quilt those pieces as a whole. In this block, the quilting overlapped two strips.

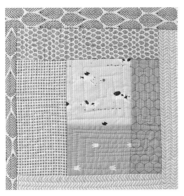

Front of block with overlap quilting

Back of block with overlap quilting

Individual Quilting

Quilt each strip individually right after you sew it onto the block. In most cases, the quilting is simple straight lines parallel to the seam.

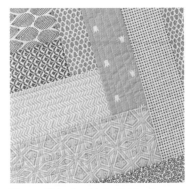

Front of block with individual quilting

Back of block with individual quilting

Combination Quilting

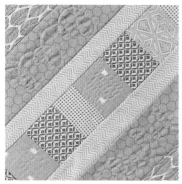

This block has a combination of straight-line quilting, no quilting (yellow strips), and free-motion quilting. I did all the straight-line quilting first and skipped the pieces where I planned to do free-motion quilting. When I finished the straight-line quilting, I switched to a free-motion darning foot and quilted loops on the pieces that I had skipped.

In blocks like this, I quilted the loops after piecing and straight-line quilting all the blocks.

In this example, I started with a free-motion darning foot to quilt hearts onto the center of all the blocks. Then I switched to a regular presser foot, added the rest of the patchwork strips, and quilted each individually with straight lines.

In blocks like this, I quilted all the hearts first.

ASSEMBLING QUILT-AS-YOU-GO BLOCKS

After you have quilted and squared up the blocks, you are ready to assemble the quilt top. Quilt-as-you-go blocks can be assembled either of two ways: The first is to sew them together and clip the corners; and the second is to use joining strips, which look like sashing strips in a traditionally pieced quilt. You can use either way or a combination to assemble the blocks. For both assembly methods, use a ¼˝ seam allowance.

Block-to-Block Assembly

Using this method to assemble the quilt is similar to how you would assemble a traditional quilt, with the following two exceptions:

- **Use an even-feed walking foot and always backstitch.** The even-feed walking foot will prevent the layers of batting and fabric from shifting and puckering. The backstitching will keep the seams from coming open during assembly.

- **Press seams open and trim at the corners.** Use a steam setting to press the seams open. Press the seams on the front side of the quilt as well. To prevent bulky seams on the quilt top, clip all the corners of the seams.

Trim the seam at a long angle to remove bulk at each corner.

1. Sew the blocks within each row together. Press the seams open and trim the corners.

2. Sew the rows together. Place pins at each intersection to keep the rows from shifting. Press the seams open.

3. Press the seams again, this time on the front of the quilt.

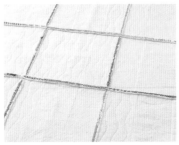

On the back, all seams are pressed open with all corners clipped

The front will look smooth, with all seams nice and flat.

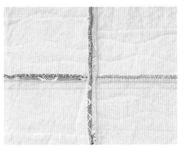

The intersections at the back of the quilt will be flat with no bulk because the corner fabric was clipped and the seams were pressed open.

Block Assembly with Joining Strips

With this method, a ½″ strip connects the blocks. The look will be similar to a sashing strip. This method is a great way to subtly frame your blocks or break up a busy pattern.

Joining strips have no batting when they are sewn onto the quilt, so you do not have to press seams open or clip corners. After the strip is sewn to a block, press the seam allowance toward the joining strip, which will back it with batting.

Blocks sewn together with joining strips

1. Cut strips 1″ × the width of fabric. Trim a strip to the length of the block. Place a joining strip on top of the block, right sides together, and align the edge of the strip with the side of the block. Stitch together, starting and ending with a backstitch. Press the seam allowance toward the joining strip.

Press the seam allowance toward the joining strip.

2. Align another block along the opposite edge of the joining strip, right sides together, and stitch. Press the seam allowance toward the joining strip.

 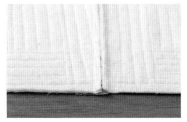

The joining strip should measure ½″ when finished.

After pressing, the joining strip will be backed with the batting from the 2 seam allowances.

3. Repeat Steps 1 and 2 to stitch each row.

4. Cut longer joining strips to match the length of a row of blocks. You may have to sew some strips together to make joining strips long enough. Repeat Steps 1 and 2 to stitch the rows together with a long joining strip between each row. You can place pins at the intersections to make sure the blocks line up.

Front of a quilt with joining strips

Back of a quilt with joining strips

Pillow Sham

BY JERA BRANDVIG

BLOCK TRIM SIZE: 16½″ × 16½″

FINISHED PILLOW: 16″ × 16″

The back of this pillow has an easy envelope closure. The design is made of strips pieced at an angle, using the quilt-as-you-go method. This block would make for a beautiful quilt, as well!

Fabric: Durham collection by Brenda Riddle for Lecien.

MATERIALS

Fabric yardages are based on 40″ usable width.
Remove selvages before cutting.

BLOCKS: ⅓ yard each of 6 coordinating fabrics for variety. You will have leftover fabric. Fat quarters will work unless you plan to make a pillow larger than 18″.

BATTING: Craft-size prepackaged batting cut 17½″ × 17½″

BACKING: ½ yard

FINDINGS: 16″ × 16″ pillow form

LIGHTWEIGHT FUSIBLE INTERFACING: 2 rectangles 12″ × 16½″ (optional)

Block Assembly

1. Using a ruler and pen, mark a diagonal line across the batting square as shown. This line will divide the block into an upper half and a lower half.

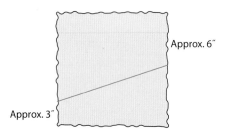

Approx. 6″

Approx. 3″

2. Cut a fabric square approximately 9″ × 9″. Align the square on the lower left end of the diagonal line, making sure it covers the lower left corner of the batting.

3. Cut a strip approximately 9″ × 13″. Position it wrong side up at a slight slant to the left so that it fans out. Before sewing it in place, preview its position to see that it will cover the lower right corner of the batting and overlap the diagonal line when attached. Sew. Trim excess fabric from the first strip. Press open and trim the excess fabric above the diagonal line.

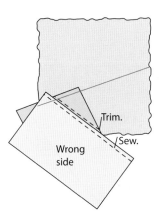

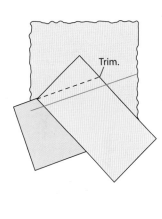

4. Add a strip approximately 9″ × 11″ as you did in Step 3, making sure it covers the rest of the bottom section of batting. Press open and trim the excess fabric above the diagonal line. Also trim the excess fabric outside the perimeter of the batting square. Quilt the lower half as desired.

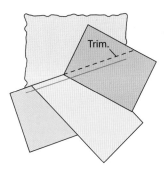

5. To fill the upper half of the batting, cut 3 rectangles approximately 5″ × 22″ each. Add a rectangle parallel with the diagonal line. Remember, the diagonal will be covered, so simply eyeball it. Sew and press open.

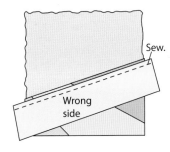

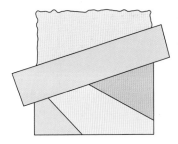

6. Add a second rectangle, previewing its position before sewing to be sure it fans outward and extends beyond the batting at both ends. Trim excess fabric from the first rectangle. Press open.

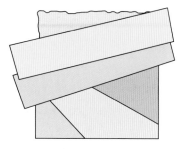

7. Add the last rectangle, positioning it to cover the rest of the batting.

8. With the batting side up, trim the excess fabric around the batting square. Quilt the top half as desired.

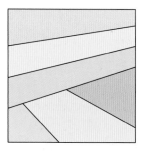

SQUARE UP YOUR BLOCK

Square up the block to 16½″ using the grid on your cutting mat. Trim a little from 2 adjacent sides of your block to create a 90° angle in a corner of the block. Align the trimmed sides with lines on your cutting mat and trim the other 2 sides.

Finish the Pillow

1. From backing fabric, cut 2 rectangles 12″ × 16½″. If you're using cotton fabric and want it to be home decorating weight, iron light-weight interfacing onto both backing rectangles.

2. Turn under ¼″ along a 16½″ edge of both rectangles. Press. Turn under an additional 1″. Press. Topstitch ¼″ from each folded edge on both rectangles.

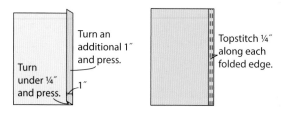

Turn an additional 1″ and press.

Turn under ¼″ and press.

1″

Topstitch ¼″ along each folded edge.

3. With right sides together, place a backing rectangle on the right side of the pillow cover, with the top-stitched edge at the center of the pillow. Sew around the raw edges, starting and ending with a back-stitch. Repeat with the other rectangle on the left side of the pillow.

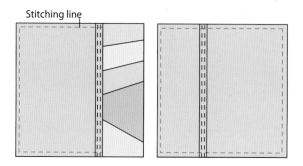

Stitching line

4. Trim the bulky fabric at the corners and turn right side out through the envelope opening. Press.

Improvisational Piecing

BY JEAN WELLS

This intuitive angle piecing exercise will help you get the feel for improvisational (improv) quilting if you have not tried it before.

With this technique, you can create interesting angles within pieced strips or in borders. Angles add interest in the composition or work as small accents in borders. I like to use strong color or higher-contrast color in the smaller pieces.

To begin thinking about a composition, make a small sketch, or cut pieces of fabric and pin them to a design wall to get a feel for the shapes you want and the color sequence. This preview will help you see where your colors will be and the proportion of colors to use.

Pillow with intuitive angle piecing

1. To begin your piecing, cut fabric pieces 1″ wider and 1″–2″ longer than the finished piece will be. This extra fabric is needed because of the angles

that will be cut and sewn. You will trim off the excess fabric later. *Always work with the right side of the fabrics facing up toward you.*

2. There are two ways to make the angle cuts.

Method 1 Place the straight edge of the ruler on the strip at the angle you wish and ¼″ beyond where you want the seam to be. Cut the angle, and remove the excess fabric. Place the second fabric under the first fabric, and use the angle you just cut as the pattern for the second cut. Place the ruler on top of the first cut, line up the angle, and cut the second fabric.

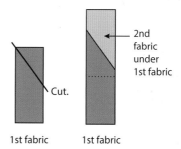

Method 2 Overlap the 2 strips. Place the ruler on top of the 2 strips, making sure that the second fabric is completely under where you are going to cut. Cut the angle, making sure the ruler is ¼″ beyond where you want the seam to be. Pull the excess fabric away from the bottom and top strips.

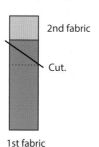

3. To stitch the seam, place the fabrics right sides together. If it is not a true 45° angle, you won't have the little triangular pieces of fabric sticking out at each end of the seam. If so, don't worry about it—you have cut the fabric a little wider and longer to begin with, so it can be trimmed. What is important is to get the angle you want in the piecing.

I have used this technique in strip piecing as well as for small inserts in Log Cabin strips on more contemporary quilts. It is a way for me to add interest to the composition.

Another option is to stitch a strip of fabric to the piecing: Place the ruler on the strip at an angle, taking into consideration seam allowances; slice at an angle.

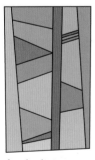

Angle slicing

Drafting a Quilt Pattern

BY SALLY COLLINS

TOOLS AND SUPPLIES

The tools you use to draft are important to the success of the process and will reflect the work you do.

Drafting tools and supplies

1. Accurate cross-section graph paper in 4-, 8-, and 10-to-the-inch increments—I use both 8½″ × 11″ and 17″ × 22″ tablets. If your designs are larger, you can tape sheets of graph paper together.

2. Compass that holds its position

3. Yardstick compass for designs larger than the span of your compass

4. Mechanical pencil

5. Good eraser, such as a white art eraser or gum eraser

6. Rulers: 1″ × 6″, 2″ × 12″, and/or 2″ × 18″ red-lined see-through rulers—I recommend the rulers from The C-Thru Ruler Company. These rulers are preferred over rotary cutting rulers for drafting because they are thin and lay flat to the paper.

7. Protractor: half-circle and full-circle—The full-circle protractor makes it much easier to draft circles.

8. Colored pencils (*optional*): 6 different colors (red, blue, orange, green, yellow, and aqua) to clarify and distinguish different drafting lines

9. Handheld calculator

10. Mirrors for designing

GRID-BASED BLOCKS

Grid Formation

Grid formation simply means that the size of the square on which you will develop your design is divided into an equal number of grids across and down. Many patchwork blocks and designs are developed on a grid of equal-sized squares across and down, much like a checkerboard. The first thing you need to learn on your journey to creative freedom is how to determine which grid you should base a particular block on. This is important because you draw the grid first, and then you use the grid to add additional lines to draw the block.

The four grid-based families in patchwork are four-patch, nine-patch, five-patch, and seven-patch.

FOUR-PATCH DRAFTING CATEGORY

For example, a block in the four-patch family can be divided into 4 equal divisions (2 × 2 grid formation). If you divide each grid in half vertically and horizontally, you have 16 equal divisions (4 × 4 grid formation); or if you divide the grids in half again, you have 64 equal divisions (8 × 8 grid formation); and so on. Each grid formation is in the four-patch family because the total number of equal divisions is divisible by 4, and the divisions are multiples of 4 (4, 16, 64).

NINE-PATCH DRAFTING CATEGORY

The math is the same for the nine-patch family. The square can have 9 equal divisions (3 × 3 grid formation); 36 equal divisions (6 × 6 grid formation); or, if divided in half again, 144 equal divisions (12 × 12 grid formation). The total number of equal divisions (9, 36, 144) is divisible by 9, and the divisions are multiples of 9.

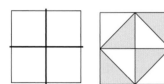

2 × 2 grid formation; 4 equal divisions

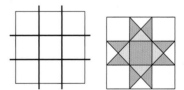

3 × 3 grid formation; 9 equal divisions

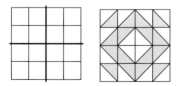

4 × 4 grid formation; 16 equal divisions

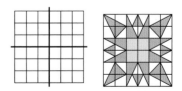

6 × 6 grid formation; 36 equal divisions

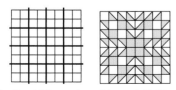

8 × 8 grid formation; 64 equal divisions

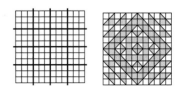

12 × 12 grid formation; 144 equal divisions

FIVE-PATCH DRAFTING CATEGORY

The five-patch family is different in that the square is divided into a 5 × 5 grid formation, or 25 equal divisions, not into 5 pieces. The square can, however, be divided as explained with four-patch and nine-patch, for example, into 100 equal divisions (10 × 10 grid formation). The total number of equal divisions is divisible by 5, and the divisions are multiples of 5.

SEVEN-PATCH DRAFTING CATEGORY

The seven-patch family is similar to the five-patch in that the square is not divided into 7 pieces but rather into a 7 × 7 grid formation with 49 equal divisions, or into a 14 × 14 grid formation with 196 equal divisions. The total number of equal divisions is divisible by 7, and the divisions are multiples of 7.

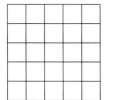

5 × 5 grid formation; 25 equal divisions

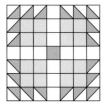 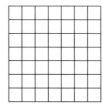

7 × 7 grid formation; 49 equal divisions

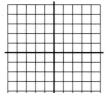 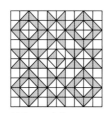

10 × 10 grid formation; 100 equal divisions

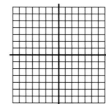 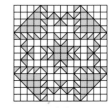

14 × 14 grid formation; 196 equal divisions

HOW TO DETERMINE THE UNDERLYING GRID FORMATION

Remember that a grid formation is based on equal-sized squares. To help recognize and determine into which grid formation a block falls, try one or more of the following options.

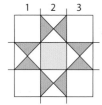

Option 1: Count the number of equal divisions across the top or side edge of a block.

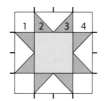

Option 2: Count the number of equal divisions along an edge-to-edge seam.

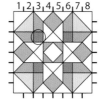

Option 3: Identify the smallest piece and count.

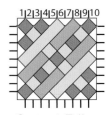

Option 4: Follow equidistant intersections, although they may not be in the same row.

Once the square has been drawn and divided into the appropriate grid formation (5 × 5, 6 × 6, 8 × 8, 7 × 7, and so on), the design is drafted by referencing your photo or sketch as you connect corners and midpoints, drawing lines to previous intersections or erasing lines over the grid. This creates shapes such as rectangles, triangles, parallelograms, trapezoids, and diamonds that are superimposed over the grid. Nothing is random or arbitrary. Erase all unneeded lines so that the remaining lines are seamlines. Shapes can occupy the space of only one grid or of multiple grids. Larger shapes are often the size of multiples of the smallest shape.

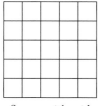

Square with grid formation

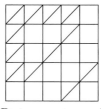

Design superimposed over grid

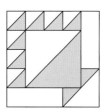

Seamlines remain.

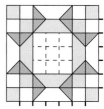

Center square occupies (and is the size of) three grids.

LET'S START DRAFTING

Once you are able to recognize the underlying grid formation of patchwork blocks, its time to test the waters. I invite you to assemble your graph paper, rulers, pencil, and eraser and join me as I go through the sequential steps of drafting a grid-based block. Reading the text and looking at the illustrations and photos, although important, will not give you necessary hands-on experience. Doing is the key to learning, knowing, and understanding.

NOTE *Whenever you draft, design, calculate, or figure out anything in patchwork, you never include seam allowance until you're ready for fabric.*

Please read through this entire section before you start. You will not actually use paper, pencil, and ruler until Step 6 (page 158).

1. Get out all tools, rulers, and graph paper (page 154).

2. Choose a pattern or block design. We will draft a Sawtooth Star.

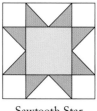

Sawtooth Star

3. Determine its drafting category and underlying grid formation.

4. Decide the size of the block. Although quilt blocks can be drafted in any size you desire (see How to Draft Any Size Square into Any Size Grid, page 160), it is easiest

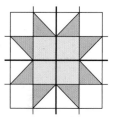

Sawtooth Star, four-patch drafting category, 4 × 4 grid formation, 16 equal divisions

to choose a size that is equally divisible by the basic grid. For example, the Sawtooth Star is drafted on a 4 × 4 grid, so it is easily drafted in any size square that is obviously equally divisible by 4 (4″, 6″, 8″, 12″). We will draft a 6″ Sawtooth Star.

NOTE *Don't forget about less obvious block sizes. For example:*

A 5″ block ÷ 4 = 1¼″ grid.

A 5½″ block ÷ 4 = 1.375 or 1⅜″ grid.

5. Determine the grid dimension (the size of each individual grid) by dividing the block size by its number of equal divisions. For our example, 6″ block ÷ 4 equal divisions = 1½″ grid dimension. I use a small handheld calculator for all my "figuring out." If your answer is not a whole number, translate three decimal places into fractions or tenths to determine which graph paper to use (10-to-the-inch or 8-to-the-inch). Knowing the grid dimension not only gives you the information you need to draw the grid but also allows you to measure your patchwork as you sew (see Using Grid Dimension to Measure Patchwork, next page).

6. Draw the chosen size of square (6″) on 8-to-the-inch graph paper and lightly draw the grid formation within the square. Here's where, together, we put pencil to paper and walk through the door to creative freedom!

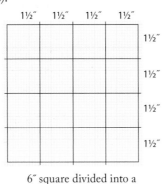

6″ square divided into a 4 × 4 grid at 1½″ intervals

NOTE *You could easily change the size of your block by changing (or choosing) the grid dimension. For example, if your grid dimension is 2″, you would multiply 2″ (grid dimension) by the number of equal divisions (4), which yields an 8″ block. If the grid is 1¼″, you would have a 5″ block; if the grid dimension is 3″, you would have a 12″ block. Multiplying the grid dimension by the number of equal divisions determines the size of the block.*

7. Develop the block design by connecting and erasing lines to subdivide the grid into shapes such as rectangles, trapezoids, parallelograms, diamonds,

and so forth. Refer to your photo or sketch until the design is complete. Begin with the largest shapes; the smaller ones will develop and become apparent. When you are finished drafting the block, erase all lines that are not seams (not all grid lines are seamlines). You should have only seamlines remaining.

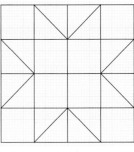

Subdivide the grid into the Sawtooth Star.

8. Identify the different shapes needed to sew the block and add their grainlines. Keep the straight of grain on the outside edges of the block. In the Sawtooth Star, there are 4 shapes: 2 right-angle triangles (1 large and 1 smaller) and 2 squares (1 large and 1 smaller). These are shapes A, B, C, and D. For stability, it's important that the straight of grain be placed on the outside edge of blocks. However, I never sacrifice design for straight grain. If there is a particular area of a fabric I want to place within a shape and it results in bias at the edge of the block or shape, I just sew and press carefully.

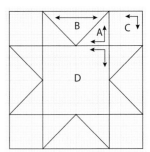

Identify the shapes and place grainlines.

9. Examine the design and determine the logical sewing sequence to piece and press the block. One way to do this is to first find the longest lines that identify a row (usually, but not always, they will run from edge to edge horizontally, vertically, or diagonally). Blocks are usually assembled by first joining pieces into units, then units into rows, then rows into the completed block.

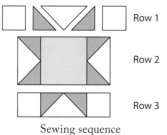

Sewing sequence

10. Isolate each individual shape, add a ¼″ seam allowance on all sides, and use your favorite cutting and sewing techniques for assembly. This step allows you to sew the design properly. When measuring a shape for cutting, if the dimensions are easily found on the ruler, then rotary cutting is the method preferred by most quilters. However, if the cutting dimensions are not easily found on the ruler, or if you want to custom cut a shape from a particular area of a fabric, make a template for that shape.

How to Determine Grid Dimension

Many square patchwork blocks are developed on a grid of equal divisions across and down a square. *Grid dimension*, which refers to the finished size of each individual grid square, determines the block size. Knowing the block's grid dimension will also allow you to measure your patchwork as you sew.

To measure your work as you sew, you must first know the grid dimension. You can determine this information in one of two ways.

- Choose the block pattern you want to sew (for example, Sawtooth Star), identify the underlying grid formation (4 × 4),

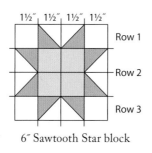

6″ Sawtooth Star block

and choose a block size (6″). To determine the grid dimension, simply divide the size of the block by the number of equal divisions across the block. For example, 6″ (block size) ÷ 4 (number of equal divisions across the block) = 1½″ grid dimension.

- Another way to determine the grid dimension of a block is to choose it. For example, let's say you want to make a Sawtooth Star block (four-patch, 4 × 4 grid formation), and you are comfortable sewing in a 1″ finished grid. The block size is determined by multiplying the grid dimension (1″) by the number of equal divisions across the block (4), so 1″ × 4 = 4″ block size. I sometimes choose the grid dimension if I'm making only one block or if I'm doing a repeat-block quilt, because then the size of the block is not as important as working in a grid dimension that I'm comfortable with.

If the grid dimension plus seam allowance is not ruler-friendly (the smallest fraction I use with rulers is ¹⁄₁₆) and I'm using templates for cutting, I use the template to evaluate and monitor the patchwork.

Using Grid Dimension to Measure Patchwork

Let's assume that we're going to sew the 6″ Sawtooth Star block that has a grid dimension of 1½″ (remember, the grid dimension does not include seam allowances).

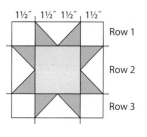

The fabric is cut (including seam allowances), the pieces and units are created, the block is laid out, and we are ready to sew together the first two pieces of Row 1.

To measure your work, follow these steps:

1. Add the number of grids you have sewn together (in this case, 3).

NOTE *When measuring, whenever a shape or unit takes up the space of more than one grid, it gets credit for the number of grids it occupies.*

2. Multiply the number of grids sewn (3) by the grid dimension (1½˝).

3. Add ½˝ for seam allowance, always. This means that for the Sawtooth Star block, 3 grids × 1½˝ = 4½˝ + ½˝ for seam

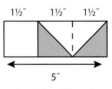

3 grids of Row 1

allowances = 5˝. The first 3 grids of Row 1 should measure 5˝ from edge to edge. If they do, great; if they do not, either the cutting or the sewing is in question. Do not continue adding grids until the first 3 measure 5˝. When these 3 grids measure 5˝, forget this number and continue.

4. Add the next piece of Row 1 to those already sewn. Because you have

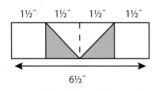

Row 1 complete

now added another grid, you must repeat Steps 1–3 to measure your work from edge to edge. The piece should now measure 6½˝ (4 grids × 1½˝ grid dimension = 6˝ + ½˝ for seam allowances = 6½˝).

Now you can draw and sew any grid-based block in any size you need!

HOW TO DRAFT ANY SIZE SQUARE INTO ANY SIZE GRID

BY SALLY COLLINS

Sometimes the size of the block you want or need will not be easily divisible by the grid of the block design. For example, to draft a 6˝ Bear's Paw block, which is a 7 × 7 grid formation, you need to divide a 6˝ square by 7. On a calculator, 6 ÷ 7 = 0.857, which is not a ruler-friendly number and which, unless you have 7-to-the-inch graph paper, is challenging to draft accurately. The following, long-standing technique drafts any size square into any size grid. The size of your square does not need to be a whole number (12˝, 8˝, and so on); it can be any size you wish (11⅜˝, 7⅝˝, 9³⁄₁₆˝, and so on).

NOTE *You can use plain or graph paper for this technique; however, I always use 8-to-the-inch graph paper. Although the drawn grid lines will not usually be on the blue graph paper lines, I use the graph paper lines in concert with the horizontal and vertical red lines of the C-Thru ruler to ensure that the grid lines I draw are exactly straight (the red line grid of the ruler is also in eighths). This drafting technique is simple in theory, but great care must be taken to ensure that all drawn grid lines are straight, accurate, and at a perfect right angle to the square's top and bottom lines. If they are not straight, the individual squares within the grid will not all be the same size or shape. Step 5 explains in detail how I use the C-Thru ruler and graph paper together.*

1. Draw the size square you desire (in this case, 6˝ × 6˝) on 8-to-the-inch graph paper. Label the 4 corners 1, 2, 3, and 4.

2. Find a measurement on your ruler that is larger than the block size and divisible by 7 (the number of equal divisions across and down). That would be the 7″ mark on your ruler. 7 is divisible by 7 and is larger than the 6″ block you chose (7″ ÷ 7 = 1″).

3. Position the corner of your ruler on the left bottom corner (#1) of your 6″ × 6″ square. Angle the ruler up until the 7″ mark on the ruler is exactly on the right side line of the 6″ square.

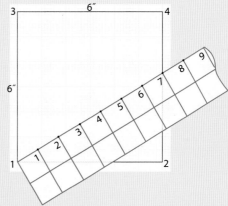

NOTES ▸

- *Another option is to place the 1″ mark of the ruler in the corner and add 1″ to the number placed on the right side line of the square (8″). If you employ this option, do not forget to add the 1″ to the number on the right side.*

- *If the number you need does not fit on the square, just extend the right edge line up to allow the ruler to reach the desired number. For example a 9″ block ÷ 7 = 1.2857. The next whole number evenly divisible by 7 is 14. 14 ÷ 7 = 2. Mark every 2″, and then draw vertical grid lines. When you rotate the paper to get the horizontal lines, extend the right edge line again.*

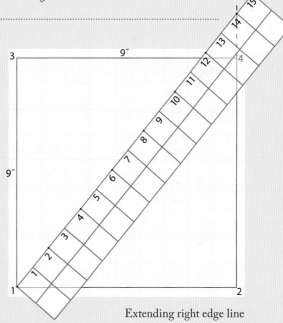

Extending right edge line

4. Mark a dot on your paper every 1″ (this is the number you arrived at by dividing 7 into 7 in Step 3). Mark dots exactly, not casually, angling your pencil lead inward, close to the ruler's edge.

5. Draw the first set of grid lines using the dots, blue graph paper lines, and the C-Thru ruler's red lines as follows:

    a. Starting at the first dot on the right side of the square (or on the left side if you are left handed), position the ruler edge next to the

dot, allowing for the width of the pencil lead. The line you will draw must travel through the center of the dot.

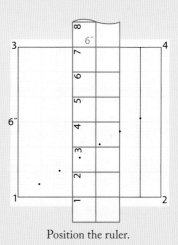

Position the ruler.

b. Now move the ruler slightly up or down and align a horizontal red line of the ruler over both the top and bottom lines of the square. If your square size is in ¹⁄₁₆ of an inch, to ensure that you're drawing an exact straight line, be sure the red lines of the ruler are equidistant from and parallel to the blue lines of the graph paper.

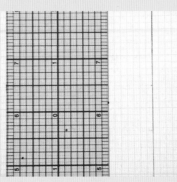

Close-up of red ruler lines and graph paper blue lines

c. Holding the ruler in place and focusing on one blue line, look through the ruler and check that the blue vertical lines of the graph paper and the red lines of the ruler are equidistant from each other from the top of the square to the bottom. If they are not, adjust the ruler so they are and then draw the line. Repeat this process for each dot.

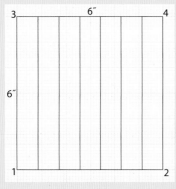

Draw grid lines.

6. Turn your paper a quarter turn and repeat Steps 3–5 (page 161) to complete the 7 × 7 grid in the 6″ × 6″ square. This grid will allow you to draft the Bear's Paw block or any seven-patch block that is 6″ × 6″.

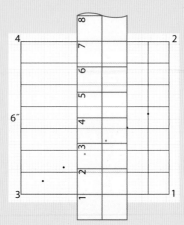

Dividing a 6″ × 6″ square into a 7 × 7 grid

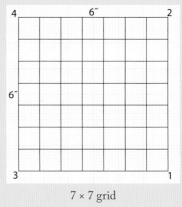

7 × 7 grid

Chapter 8:
For Your Reference

Bed/Quilt Sizes

BED, COMFORTER, COVERLET, AND BEDSPREAD MEASUREMENTS

Bed	Mattress size (inches)	Comforter (inches)	Coverlet (inches)	Bedspread (inches)
Crib	27 × 52	—	—	—
Youth	32 × 66	56 × 78	64 × 92	74 × 97
Studio/cot	30 × 75	54 × 87	62 × 101	72 × 106
Bunk	38 × 75	62 × 87	70 × 101	80 × 106
Twin	39 × 75	63 × 87	71 × 101	81 × 106
Twin, XL	39 × 80	63 × 92	71 × 106	81 × 111
Twin, wide	48 × 75	72 × 87	80 × 101	90 × 106
Double/full	54 × 75	78 × 87	86 × 101	96 × 106
Double, XL	54 × 80	78 × 92	86 × 106	96 × 111
Queen	60 × 80	84 × 92	92 × 106	102 × 111
California king	72 × 84	96 × 96	104 × 110	114 × 115
King	78 × 80	102 × 92	110 × 106	120 × 111

NOTE: Comforters cover the mattress but not the box spring and generally don't have a pillow tuck. Coverlets cover the mattress and box spring and generally have a pillow tuck. Bedspreads cover the bed to almost the floor and have a pillow tuck.

QUILT SIZES WITH DROP AND TUCK

Added drop and tuck		Twin (inches) 39 × 75	Double/full (inches) 54 × 75	Queen (inches) 60 × 80	King (inches) 78 × 80
Drop*	Tuck**				
10″	—	59 × 85	74 × 85	80 × 90	98 × 90
10″	10″	59 × 95	74 × 95	80 × 100	98 × 100
12″	—	63 × 87	78 × 87	84 × 92	102 × 92
12″	10″	63 × 97	78 × 97	84 × 102	102 × 102
14″	—	67 × 89	82 × 89	88 × 94	106 × 94
14″	10″	67 × 99	82 × 99	88 × 104	106 × 104
16″	—	71 × 91	86 × 91	92 × 96	110 × 96
16″	10″	71 × 101	86 × 101	92 × 106	110 × 106
18″	—	75 × 93	90 × 93	96 × 98	114 × 98
18″	10″	75 × 103	90 × 103	96 × 108	114 × 108
20″	—	79 × 95	94 × 95	100 × 100	118 × 100
20″	10″	79 × 105	94 × 105	100 × 110	118 × 110
22″	—	83 × 97	98 × 97	104 × 102	122 × 102
22″	10″	83 × 107	98 × 107	104 × 112	122 × 112

* Drop hangs over the edge of the mattress on 3 sides.
** Tuck folds under the pillow.

CUSTOMIZING QUILT SIZE

Referring to the bed illustration and formulas, use your own bed measurements to determine the size quilt you need.

A = distance from top to dust ruffle

B = distance from top to floor

L = mattress length

W = mattress width

T = mattress thickness

PT = pillow tuck allowance (approx. 10″)

CR = contraction rate (quilt and batting shrinkage: 3%–5%)

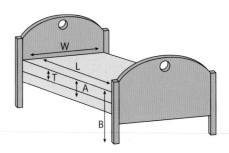

BY HARRIET HARGRAVE AND SHARYN CRAIG

Quilt type	Width	Length
Blanket (4″ tuck allowance)	W + 2T + 8″ + CR	L + 1T + 4″ + CR
Comforter	W + 2T + CR	L + 1A + CR
Coverlet (tucked under pillow)	W + 2A + CR	L + 1A + PT + CR
Bedspread	W + 2B + CR	L + 1B + PT + CR

For more detailed information, see The Art of Classic Quiltmaking by Harriet Hargrave and Sharyn Craig (available as a Print-On-Demand or eBook from C&T Publishing).

Yardage Requirements

Keep the following charts handy when cutting fabric yardage.
(For instructions, see Rotary Cutting Basics, page 33.)

YARDAGE FOR SQUARES

Cut size (inches)	Yardage							
	¼	½	¾	1	1¼	1½	1¾	2
1	360	720	1,080	1,440	1,800	2,160	2,520	2,880
1½	156	312	468	624	780	936	1,092	1,248
2	80	180	260	360	440	540	620	720
2½	48	112	160	224	288	336	400	448
3	39	78	117	156	195	236	273	312
3½	22	44	77	110	132	165	198	220
4	20	40	60	90	110	130	150	180
4½	18	36	54	72	90	108	126	144
5	8	24	40	56	72	80	96	112
5½	7	21	28	42	56	63	77	91
6	6	18	24	36	42	54	60	72
6½	6	12	24	30	36	48	54	66
7	5	10	15	25	30	35	45	50
7½	5	10	15	20	30	35	40	45
8	5	10	15	20	25	30	35	45
8½	4	8	12	16	20	24	28	32
9	4	8	12	16	20	24	28	32
9½		4	8	12	16	20	24	28
10		4	8	12	16	20	24	28
10½		3	6	9	12	18	15	18
11		3	6	9	12	12	15	18
11½		3	6	9	9	12	15	18
12		3	6	9	9	12	15	18

NOTE: Yardage amounts are based on 42″ fabric width. If your fabric is wider or narrower than 42″, make adjustments accordingly. • We advise purchasing ⅛ yard extra to allow for variations in cutting.

YARDAGE FOR RECTANGLES

Cut size (inches; width × length)	Yardage							
	¼	½	¾	1	1¼	1½	1¾	2
1½ × 2½	96	192	288	384	480	576	672	768
1½ × 3½	66	132	198	264	330	396	462	528
1½ × 4½	54	108	162	216	270	324	378	432
2 × 3½	44	88	143	198	242	297	341	396
2 × 4½	36	81	117	162	198	243	279	324
2½ × 3½	33	66	110	154	198	231	275	308
2½ × 4½	27	63	90	126	162	189	225	252
2½ × 5½	21	49	70	98	126	147	175	196
2½ × 6½	18	42	60	84	108	126	150	168
3 × 4½	27	54	81	108	135	162	189	216
3 × 5½	21	42	63	84	105	126	147	168
3 × 6½	18	36	54	72	90	108	126	144
3½ × 4½	18	45	63	90	108	135	162	180
3½ × 5½	14	35	49	70	84	105	126	140
3½ × 6½	12	30	42	60	72	90	108	120
3½ × 7½	10	25	35	50	60	75	90	100
4 × 5½	14	28	42	63	77	91	105	126
4 × 6½	12	24	36	54	66	78	90	108
4 × 7½	10	20	30	45	55	65	75	90
4½ × 5½	14	28	42	56	70	84	98	112
4½ × 6½	12	24	36	48	60	72	84	96
4½ × 7½	10	20	30	40	50	60	70	80
5 × 6½	6	18	30	42	54	60	72	84
5 × 7½	5	15	25	35	45	50	60	70
5½ × 6½	6	18	24	36	48	54	66	78
5½ × 7½	5	15	20	30	40	45	55	65
5½ × 8½	4	12	16	24	32	36	44	52

NOTE: Yardage amounts are based on 42˝ fabric width. If your fabric is wider or narrower than 42˝, make adjustments accordingly. • Numbers are based on cutting strips (selvage to selvage) the width measurement and then cutting the strips into rectangles the length measurement. • We advise purchasing ⅛ yard extra to allow for variations in cutting.

YARDAGE FOR SASHING STRIPS

Cut size (inches; width × length)	Yardage							
	¼	½	¾	1	1¼	1½	1¾	2
1½ × 4½	54	108	162	216	270	324	378	432
1½ × 5½	42	84	126	168	210	252	294	336
1½ × 6½	36	72	108	144	180	216	252	288
1½ × 8½	24	48	72	96	120	144	168	192
1½ × 9½	24	48	72	96	120	144	168	192
1½ × 10½	18	36	54	72	90	108	126	144
1½ × 12½	18	36	54	72	90	108	126	144
2 × 5½	28	63	91	126	154	189	217	252
2 × 6½	24	54	78	108	132	162	186	216
2 × 8½	16	36	52	72	88	108	124	144
2 × 9½	16	36	52	72	88	108	124	144
2 × 10½	12	27	39	54	66	81	93	108
2 × 12½	12	27	39	54	66	81	93	108
2½ × 5½	21	49	70	98	126	147	175	196
2½ × 6½	18	42	60	84	108	126	150	168
2½ × 8½	12	28	40	56	72	84	100	112
2½ × 9½	12	28	40	56	72	84	100	112
2½ × 10½	9	21	30	42	54	63	75	84
2½ × 12½	9	21	30	42	54	63	75	84
3 × 6½	18	36	54	72	90	108	126	144
3 × 8½	12	24	36	48	60	72	84	96
3 × 9½	12	24	36	48	60	72	84	96
3 × 10½	9	18	27	36	45	54	63	72
3 × 12½	9	18	27	36	45	54	63	72
3½ × 6½	12	30	42	60	72	90	108	120
3½ × 8½	8	20	28	40	48	60	72	80
3½ × 9½	8	20	28	40	48	60	72	80
3½ × 10½	6	15	21	30	36	45	54	60
3½ × 12½	6	15	21	30	36	45	54	60

NOTE: Yardage amounts are based on 42˝ fabric width. If your fabric is wider or narrower than 42˝, make adjustments accordingly. • Numbers are based on cutting strips (selvage to selvage) the width measurement and then cutting the strips into rectangles the length measurement. • We advise purchasing ⅛ yard extra to allow for variations in cutting.

YARDAGE FOR BORDERS CUT ON CROSSWISE* GRAIN

Quilt size before borders (inches; width × length)	Border width (cut width in inches)													
	1½˝	2˝	2½˝	3˝	3½˝	4˝	4½˝	5˝	5½˝	6˝	6½˝	7˝	8˝	9˝
24 × 24	¼	⅓	⅜	½	½	⅝	⅝	¾	—	—	—	—	—	—
24 × 36	¼	⅓	⅜	½	½	⅔	¾	⅞	—	—	—	—	—	—
36 × 48	¼	⅓	½	⅝	¾	⅞	⅞	1	1⅛	1¼	1⅓	1⅜	—	—
38 × 52	⅓	½	½	⅝	¾	⅞	⅞	1	1⅛	1¼	1⅓	1⅝	—	—
48 × 60	⅓	½	⅝	⅔	⅞	1	1	1⅛	1¼	1⅓	1½	1⅝	2	2¼
52 × 52	⅓	½	½	⅝	⅞	1	1	1⅛	1¼	1⅓	1½	1⅝	1⅞	2¼
58 × 62	⅓	½	⅝	⅔	⅞	1	1⅛	1¼	1⅜	1½	1⅝	1¾	2	2¼
60 × 72	⅜	½	⅝	¾	⅞	1	1⅛	1¼	1⅜	1½	1⅝	2	2¼	2½
62 × 86	⅜	½	⅝	⅞	1	1⅛	1¼	1½	1⅝	1⅔	1⅞	2	2½	2¾
62 × 92	½	⅝	¾	⅞	1	1⅛	1¼	1½	1⅝	1⅔	2	2¼	2½	2¾
69 × 96	½	⅝	¾	⅞	1	1¼	1⅜	1⅝	1¾	1⅞	2	2¼	2½	3
76 × 110	½	⅝	⅞	1	1⅛	1⅓	1½	1⅔	1⅞	2	2¼	2⅓	2⅔	3¼
86 × 115	½	⅔	⅞	1	1¼	1⅓	1½	1⅔	2	2¼	2⅜	2⅝	3	3¼
96 × 110	½	⅔	⅞	1	1¼	1½	1⅝	1⅞	2	2¼	2⅜	2⅝	3	3¼
106 × 116	⅝	¾	1	1⅛	1⅓	1½	1⅝	1⅞	2¼	2⅓	2⅝	2¾	3⅛	3½

NOTE: Yardage amounts are based on 42˝ fabric width. Extra fabric has been allowed for 1 extra strip and mitered corners (formula: twice the border cut width + 5˝).

* Crosswise grain is selvage to selvage.

YARDAGE FOR BORDERS CUT ON LENGTHWISE* GRAIN

Quilt size before borders (inches; width × length)	Border width (cut width in inches)				
	1½″–2½″	3″–4½″	5″–6½″	7″–8½″	9″–10″
24 × 24	1	1⅛	1¼	—	—
24 × 36	1⅓	1⅜	1⅝	—	—
30 × 40	1⅜	1⅝	1⅔	1¾	—
36 × 48	1⅔	1¾	1⅞	2	—
38 × 52	1¾	1⅞	2	2⅛	—
48 × 54	1⅞	2	2⅛	2⅛	2¼
48 × 60	2	2⅛	2¼	2⅓	2½
52 × 52	1¾	1⅞	2	2⅛	2¼
56 × 68	2¼	2⅓	2½	2⅝	2⅝
58 × 62	2⅛	2¼	2⅓	2⅜	2½
60 × 72	2⅓	2½	2⅝	2⅔	2¾
60 × 80	2⅝	2⅔	2¾	2⅞	3
62 × 86	2¾	2⅞	3	3⅛	3⅛
62 × 92	3	3	3⅛	3¼	3⅜
66 × 105	3¼	3⅜	3½	3⅝	3¾
69 × 96	3	3⅛	3¼	3⅜	3½
76 × 110	3½	3½	3⅝	3¾	3⅞
86 × 105	3¼	3⅜	3½	3⅝	3¾
86 × 115	3⅝	3⅔	3¾	3⅞	4
90 × 110	3½	3½	3⅝	3¾	3⅞
96 × 110	3½	3½	3⅝	3¾	3⅞
100 × 110	3½	3½	3⅝	3¾	3⅞
106 × 116	3⅝	3¾	3⅞	4	4
112 × 110	3½	3⅝	3⅔	3⅞	3⅞
124 × 116	3¾	4	4	4⅛	4¼

* *Lengthwise grain is parallel to the selvages.*

NOTE: Yardage amounts are based on 42″ fabric width. If your fabric is wider or narrower than 42″, make adjustments accordingly. • Extra fabric has been allowed for 1 extra strip and mitered corners (Formula: twice the border cut width + 5″).

YARDAGE FOR QUILT BACKING

Backing size (inches; width × length)	Layout	Yards
28 × 28	A	1
28 × 40	A	1
34 × 44	A	1¼
40 × 52	A	1½
42 × 56	A	1⅝
48 × 54	B	2¾
48 × 60	B	2¾
52 × 52	B	3
56 × 68	B	3⅛
58 × 62	B	3¼
60 × 72	B	3⅜
60 × 80	B	3⅜
62 × 86	C	4⅞
62 × 92	C	5⅛
66 × 105	C	5⅞
69 × 96	C	5⅜
76 × 110	C	6⅛
86 × 105	D	7¼
86 × 115	D	7¼
90 × 110	D	7½
96 × 110	D	8
100 × 111	D	8⅜
106 × 116	D	8⅞
112 × 110	E	9¼
124 × 116	E	9¾

NOTE: Yardage amounts are based on 42″ fabric width and are rounded up to the nearest ⅛ yard.

- *If your fabric is wider or narrower than 42″, make adjustments accordingly.*
- **Layout A:** *We advise purchasing ⅛ yard extra to allow for variations in cutting.*
- **Layouts B–E:** *We advise purchasing ¼ yard extra to allow for variations in cutting.*
- **Layouts B and C:** *Cut the fabric in half crosswise (selvage to selvage), remove the selvages, and then sew the 2 pieces together lengthwise (along the long edges).*
- **Layouts D and E:** *Cut the fabric in thirds crosswise (selvage to selvage), remove the selvages, and then sew the 3 pieces together lengthwise (along the long edges).*

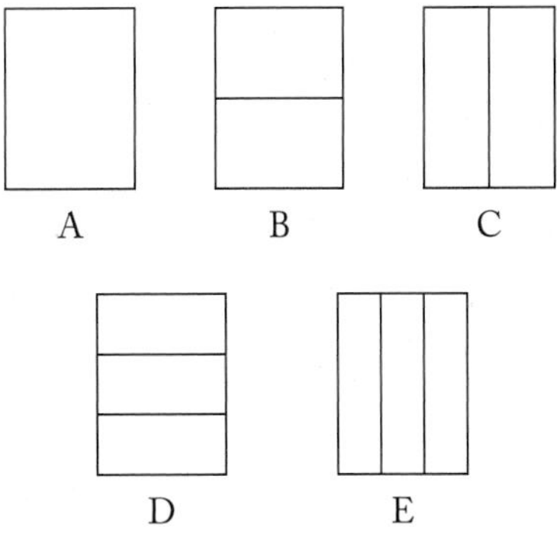

Perimeter of quilt + 10″ (inches)	No. of 1⅛″-wide strips	Yardage	No. of 1⅝″-wide strips	Yardage	No. of 2⅛″-wide strips	Yardage	No. of 2⅜″-wide strips	Yardage	No. of 3⅛″-wide strips	Yardage	No. of 4⅝″-wide strips	Yardage
80–126	3	⅛	3	¼	3	¼	3	¼	3	⅓	3	½
127–168	4	¼	4	¼	4	¼	4	⅓	4	⅜	4	⅝
169–210	5	¼	5	¼	5	⅓	5	⅓	5	½	5	⅔
211–252	6	¼	6	⅓	6	⅜	6	½	6	⅝	6	⅞
253–294	7	¼	7	⅓	7	½	7	½	7	⅝	7	1
295–336	8	⅓	8	⅜	8	½	8	⅝	8	¾	8	1⅛
337–378	9	⅓	9	½	9	⅝	9	⅝	9	⅞	9	1¼
379–420	10	⅓	10	½	10	⅝	10	¾	10	1	10	1⅓
421–462	11	⅜	11	⅝	11	¾	11	⅞	11	1	11	1½

NOTE: Yardage amounts are based on 42″ fabric width. If your fabric is wider or narrower than 42″, make adjustments accordingly.

Precut Fabrics

Keep the following information handy when cutting precut fabrics.

CUTTING FROM FAT QUARTERS (18″ × 22″)

Photo by Robert Kaufman Fabrics

Cut fat quarters into:
56 squares 2½″ × 2½″
35 squares 3″ × 3″
30 squares 3½″ × 3½″
20 squares 4″ × 4″
12 squares 4½″ × 4½″
12 squares 5″ × 5″
9 squares 5½″ × 5½″
6 squares 6″ × 6″
6 squares 6½″ × 6½″
6 squares 7″ × 7″
4 squares 7½″ × 7½″
4 squares 8″ × 8″
4 squares 8½″ × 8½″

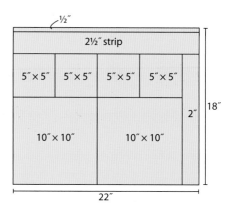

CUTTING FROM LAYER CAKES (10″ × 10″ SQUARE)

Photo by
RJR Fabrics

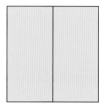

Cut in half to
get 2 rectangles
5″ × 10″.

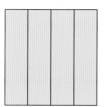

Cut into 4 strips
2½″ × 10″.

Cut into 5 strips
2″ × 10″.

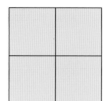

Cut in half twice
to get 4 squares
5″ × 5″.

Cut into 16 squares
2½″ × 2½″ (Mini
Charm Squares).

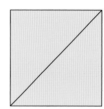

Cut diagonally
once to get 2 half-
square triangles
that once trimmed,
finish to 9″.

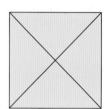

Cut diagonally
twice to get
4 quarter-square
triangles that
once trimmed,
finish to 8½″.

CUTTING FROM CHARM SQUARES (5″ × 5″ SQUARE)

Photo by
Robert Kaufman Fabrics

Cut into 4 squares
2½″ × 2½″.

Cut diagonally once
to get 2 half-square
triangles that once
trimmed, finish to 4″.

Cut diagonally twice
to get 4 quarter-square
triangles that once
trimmed, finish to 3½″.

Piecing

BY HARRIET HARGRAVE AND SHARYN CRAIG

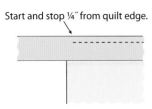

1. Pin securely and stitch strips to quilt top; start and stop stitching ¼″ from quilt edge.

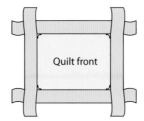

2. Press borders open and extend excess border length beyond each end.

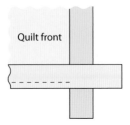

3. Position border strips for mitering.

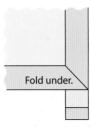

4. Fold top border strip under so it meets edge of bottom border strip and forms a 45° angle. Press the fold in place.

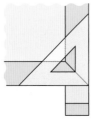

5. Pin the fold in place. Position a 90° angle ruler over corner until it is flat and square. Remove pins and press the fold firmly. Center masking tape over mitered fold.

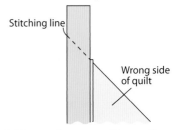

6. Turn quilt top over. Draw a line slightly outside crease. Fold center section of quilt top diagonally from corner, right sides together, and align long edges of border strips. Beginning at inside corner, backstitch and stitch on line. Backstitch at end. Remove tape, trim seam allowance to ¼″, and press seam open.

* For more detailed information, see The Art of Classic Quiltmaking by Harriet Hargrave and Sharyn Craig (available as a Print-On-Demand or eBook from C&T Publishing).

Straight-Set Quilts

NUMBER OF BLOCKS NEEDED IN STRAIGHT-SET QUILTS

Block setting	Number of blocks	Alternate set	
		Design blocks	Alternate blocks
3 × 3	9	5	4
3 × 5	15	8	7
5 × 5	25	13	12
5 × 7	35	18	17
7 × 7	49	25	24
7 × 9	63	32	31
9 × 9	81	41	40
9 × 11	99	50	49

3 × 3 setting

INCHES ADDED BY SASHING TO STRAIGHT-SET QUILTS*

BY HARRIET HARGRAVE AND SHARYN CRAIG

Sashing width (inches; finished size)	Number of blocks across or down a row								
	4	5	6	7	8	9	10	11	12
½	2½	3	3½	4	4½	5	5½	6	6½
1	5	6	7	8	9	10	11	12	13
1½	7½	9	10½	12	13½	15	16½	18	19½
2	10	12	14	16	18	20	22	24	26
2½	12½	15	17½	20	22½	25	27½	30	32½
3	15	18	21	24	27	30	33	36	39
3½	17½	21	24½	28	31½	35	38½	42	45½
4	20	24	28	32	36	40	44	48	52
4½	22½	27	31½	36	40½	45	49½	54	58½
5	25	30	35	40	45	50	55	60	65

1. Read across the top horizontal row to find the number of blocks in a horizontal row on your quilt.

2. Read down the first vertical column to find the finished size of your sashing.

3. Then, find the number on the chart where the row and the column come together. This is the size added by the sashing.

4. Repeat for the number of blocks in a vertical row on your quilt.

For more detailed information, see The Art of Classic Quiltmaking by Harriet Hargrave and Sharyn Craig (available as a Print-On-Demand or eBook from C&T Publishing).

NUMBER OF SASHING PIECES AND CORNERSTONES NEEDED FOR STRAIGHT-SET QUILTS*

BY SHARYN CRAIG

Block setting (width × length)	Number of blocks	Horizontal sashing pieces without cornerstones	Vertical sashing pieces without cornerstones	Sashing pieces with cornerstones	Cornerstones
2 × 2	4	3	6	12	9
2 × 3	6	4	9	17	12
3 × 3	9	4	12	24	16
3 × 4	12	5	16	31	20
3 × 5	15	6	20	38	24
4 × 4	16	5	20	40	25
4 × 5	20	6	25	49	30
4 × 6	24	7	30	58	35
5 × 5	25	6	30	60	36
5 × 6	30	7	36	71	42
5 × 7	35	8	42	82	48
6 × 6	36	7	42	84	49
6 × 7	42	8	49	97	56
6 × 8	48	9	56	110	63
7 × 7	49	8	56	112	64
7 × 8	56	9	64	127	72
7 × 9	63	10	72	142	80

For more detailed information, see Great Sets by Sharyn Craig (available as a Print-On-Demand or eBook from C&T Publishing).

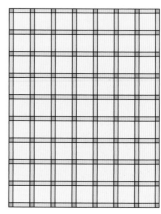

7 × 9 setting with sashing

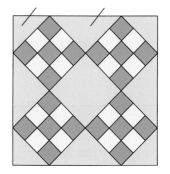

7 × 9 setting with sashing and cornerstones

Diagonal-Set Quilts

SIDE AND CORNER TRIANGLES FOR DIAGONAL SETTINGS

Finished block size	Cut squares for side triangles*	Cut squares for corner triangles**
3″	5½″	3″
4″	6⅞″	3¾″
5″	8⅜″	4½″
6″	9¾″	5⅛″
8″	12⅝″	6⅝″
9″	14″	7¼″
10″	15⅜″	8″
12″	18¼″	9⅜″
15″	22½″	11½″

*Cut in half diagonally, twice.   **Cut in half diagonally.*

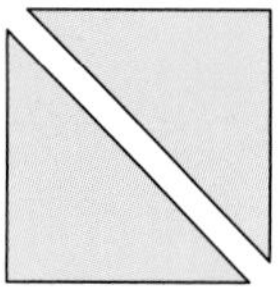

Corner triangles 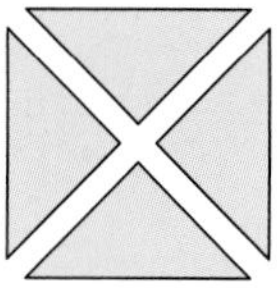   Side triangles

DIAGONAL MEASUREMENTS OF BLOCKS

Block size	Width on point
4″	5⅝″
4½″	6⅜″
5″	7¹⁄₁₆″
5½″	7¾″
6″	8½″
6½″	9³⁄₁₆″
7″	9⅞″
7½″	10⅝″
8″	11⁵⁄₁₆″
8½″	12″
9″	12¾″
9½″	13⁷⁄₁₆″
10″	14⅛″
10½″	14⅞″
11″	15⁹⁄₁₆″

Block size	Width on point
11½″	16¼″
12″	17″
12½″	17¹¹⁄₁₆″
13″	18⅜″
13½″	19¹⁄₁₆″
14″	19¹³⁄₁₆″
14½″	20½″
15″	21¼″
15½″	21¹⁵⁄₁₆″
16″	22⅝″
16½″	23⁵⁄₁₆″
17″	24¹⁄₁₆″
17½″	24¾″
18″	25⁷⁄₁₆″
18½″	26³⁄₁₆″

INCHES ADDED BY SASHING TO DIAGONAL-SET QUILTS*

BY HARRIET HARGRAVE AND SHARYN CRAIG

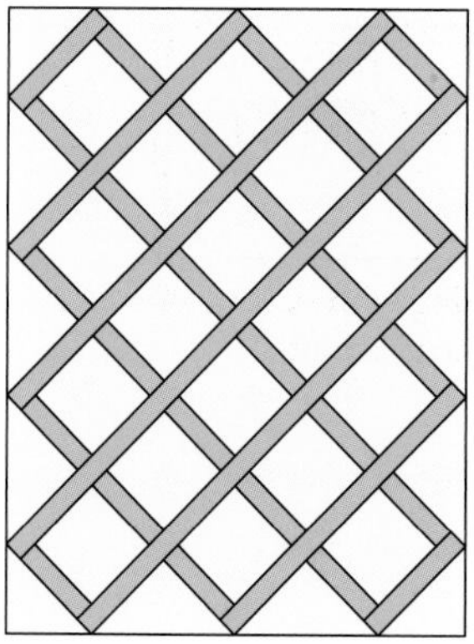

3 × 4 diagonal set with sashing

Sashing width (inches; finished size)	Number of blocks across or down a row							
	3	4	5	6	7	8	9	10
½	2⅞	3½	4¼	5	5⅝	6⅜	7⅛	7¾
1	5⅝	7⅛	8½	9⅞	11⅜	12¾	14⅛	15½
1½	8½	10⅝	12¾	14⅞	17	19⅛	21¼	23⅜
2	11⅜	14⅛	17	19¾	22⅝	25½	28¼	31⅛
2½	14⅛	17⅝	21¼	24¾	28¼	31⅞	35⅜	38⅞
3	17	21¼	25½	29¾	34	38⅛	42⅜	46⅝
3½	19¾	24¾	29¾	34⅝	39⅝	44½	49½	54½
4	22⅝	28¼	34	39⅝	45¼	51	56½	62¼

1. Read across the top horizontal row to find the number of blocks in a horizontal row on your quilt.

2. Read down the first vertical column to find the finished size of your sashing.

3. Then, find the number on the chart where the row and the column come together. This is the size added by the sashing.

4. Repeat for the number of blocks in a vertical row on your quilt.

** For more detailed information, see The Art of Classic Quiltmaking by Harriet Hargrave and Sharyn Craig (available as a Print-On-Demand or eBook from C&T Publishing).*

About the Contributors

Check out these contributor websites and books for more great content! For additional resources on patchwork and quilting by these and other authors, visit C&T Publishing at ctpub.com.

ALEX ANDERSON **alexandersonquilts.com**
Alex Anderson's Hand & Machine Appliqué
All Things Quilting with Alex Anderson
Paper Piecing with Alex Anderson, 2nd Edition
Start Quilting with Alex Anderson, 3rd Edition

JERA BRANDVIG **quiltingintherain.com**
Quilt As-You-Go Made Modern

CHRISTINA CAMELI **afewscraps.com**
First Steps to Free-Motion Quilting

ALISSA HAIGHT CARLTON **alissahaightcarlton.com**
Modern Minimal

SALLY COLLINS **sallycollins.org**
Drafting for the Creative Quilter

SHARYN CRAIG **sharyncraig.com**
All-in-One Quilter's Reference Tool,
Updated Second Edition

SUE DALEY **busyfingerspatchwork.com**
New English Paper Piecing

BECKY GOLDSMITH **pieceocake.com**
The Quilter's Practical Guide to Color

JANE HALL
Every Quilter's Foundation Piecing Reference Tool

CARRIE AND HARRIET HARGRAVE
Quilter's Academy Vol. 1—Freshman Year
Quilter's Academy Vol. 2—Sophomore Year

HARRIET HARGRAVE **harriethargrave.com**
All-in-One Quilter's Reference Tool

ELIZABETH HARTMAN **ohfransson.com**
The Practical Guide to Patchwork
Modern Patchwork

DIXIE HAYWOOD
Every Quilter's Foundation Piecing Reference Tool

SHERRI MCCONNELL **aquiltinglife.com**
A Quilting Life

JUDITH BAKER MONTANO **judithbakermontano.com**
The Crazy Quilt Handbook, Revised 3rd Edition

GINA PERKES **thecopperneedle.com**
Mastering the Art of Longarm Quilting

ANGELA WALTERS **quiltingismytherapy.com**
Free-Motion Quilting with Angela Walters

JEAN WELLS **stitchinpost.com**
Intuitive Color & Design

WENDY WILLIAMS **flyingfishkits.com.au**
Wild Blooms & Colorful Creatures

COREY YODER **littlemissshabby.com**
Playful Petals

Index